FRANK DELL
with BRETT PIPER

MOSQUITO DOWN!

The Extraordinary Memoir of a Second
World War Bomber Command Pilot on
the Run in Germany and Holland

Complete and Unabridged

PUBLISHER SELECTION
Leicester

First published in Great Britain in 2014 by
Fighting High Ltd
Hertfordshire

First Ulverscroft Edition
published 2018
by arrangement with
Fighting High Ltd
Hertfordshire

The moral right of the author has been asserted

A catalogue record for this book is available
from the British Library.

ISBN 978–1–4448–3851–0

Published by
F. A. Thorpe (Publishing)
Anstey, Leicestershire

Set by Words & Graphics Ltd.
Anstey, Leicestershire
Printed and bound in Great Britain by
T. J. International Ltd., Padstow, Cornwall

This book is printed on acid-free paper

MOSQUITO DOWN!

Frank Dell's experience as a Second World War pilot with the Royal Air Force's Light Night Striking Force takes an even more dramatic turn when his Mosquito is shot down over Germany in October 1944. Frank recounts his escape from the disintegrating aircraft by parachute, and how, battered and bruised, he finds himself in a field adjacent to a German V2 rocket launch pad. Determined to avoid capture, he crosses Nazi Germany and finds refuge in Holland with a Dutch Resistance group. He emerges from his traumatic experiences with heightened respect for the courageous Dutch families who risked death to shelter him and other Allied airmen.

Dedication

This book is dedicated to the people of the Netherlands for their stoical resistance to the enemy during the Second World War and for their generosity of spirit in helping and hiding the many hundreds of Allied airmen and airborne soldiers who found themselves in Occupied Holland through the circumstances of war. War is terrible, but through it remarkable instances of bravery and sacrifice shine brightly and the Netherlands serves as an example to us all. How can we who passed through thank them adequately.

To my navigator, Flying Officer Ron Naiff: he was my friend and I remember him every day.

Contents

Chapter 1

Shot Down

The 692 Squadron Operations Diary for the night of 14/15 October 1944 records:

A small scale attack made in clear weather. All aircraft carried a 4000lb bomb and released between 0305 and 0307 hours from 25,000–27,000 feet. The defences did not open up until the attack had developed and most crews were out of the target area before the usual intense flak started. The searchlights were also not very active. F/O F.H. Dell and F/O R.A. Naiff did not return from this sortie.

My story starts at approximately eleven o'clock on Saturday evening, 14 October 1944. Feeling very disgruntled and wondering whether in hell's name we really were going to get off this time, we, the pilots, filed into the briefing room. We glanced quickly at the large wall map bearing the route tapes, grimaced when we saw the target, and wandered over to join our respective navigators.

We had been through the same procedure the night before but our raid had been called off because of heavy cloud over the target. This had been a relief to Ron and I, as it was to have been our thirteenth trip, the date was 13 October and the day of the week was Friday! Neither of us was

1

superstitious really but it didn't seem desirable to tempt fate; I also carried in my trouser pocket a small stuffed elephant given to me by my sister-in-law to bring me good luck.

This was the third time this particular evening that we had been briefed for the trip. Firstly it had been Hamburg. Then that had been cancelled and Berlin substituted. Then that destination had been scrapped while the duty navigator had been pestering Group for upper winds. 'Why in blazes can't they make up their x–x minds,' said the wing commander and packed us all off back to our respective Messes.

So we hung about in the Mess, checked up on the latest episode of 'Jane' in the *Daily Mirror*, read the last paragraph of 'London day by day' in the *Daily Telegraph*, both guaranteed for a little chuckle, and nattered with the boys in front of the big, open fire with its logs crackling in the hearth. And waited.

I wrote a very scruffy little letter to my girlfriend Pam, using NAAFI paper. Afterwards I always regretted what I said in this letter – it must have sounded very despondent, which was not really the case, just a little keyed up. You see my navigator Ron and I were both recovering from flu-like colds, which between us had kept us off flying for about a fortnight. Ron had such a high temperature that he had been put into Ely hospital for a few days. As the night wore on we became more and more tired, heady and irritable.

At last the call came to send us back to the briefing room, the navigators having gone a little earlier to get cracking on their charts.

And there we were sitting beside our navigators listening to the commanding officer saying, 'Well chaps it's Big City again.'

This brought loud groans from the crews.

'As you can see you are routed across Holland and through the Gap.[1] Home via Hamburg. The Heavies are going to Duisburg tonight so you will be doing a feint towards their target as they are turning homewards, while you will veer north-eastwards towards Münster to draw off the night fighters from the Lancs and Halifaxes.'

This was greeted with more sarcastic groans.

'Pathfinder Force will be marking the turning points en route with green flares and the target with reds. It will be a Paramatta[2] attack. Intelligence please!'

The Intelligence King got up – a new chap that I had only seen in the Mess a day or two before that night. He might have warned us of the re-grouping of anti-aircraft (AA) or searchlights in the Gap. Or the disposition of German night-fighter squadrons. Or even the new night-fighter techniques being adopted by the Germans. However, on this occasion all he said was, 'You shouldn't encounter anything tonight that you have not experienced before.' And then he sat down. He couldn't have been more wrong.

At last we climbed into our aircraft, started up, taxied out in our given order, took off and climbed for altitude prior to setting course. We were back over the Drem lights two minutes before setting course time and just had a moment for a slightly tightened 360-degree turn before heading off and away into cloud. Five Mosquitoes from our squadron left in the space of five minutes.

Our aircraft N for Nuts climbed like a bird and, glory of glories, actually reached 23,000 feet before I put her into 'high blower'. While our planned cruising height was 27,000 feet, I went up to nearly 28,000 before easing the nose down, closing the radiator flaps, and building up to our cruising speed. The aircraft was brand spanking new and she simply slipped along. Nothing could catch us! Or so I thought.

We were going well over the North Sea and it was now that I noticed those beautiful flickering fingers of the aurora borealis – streaks of blue and mauve waving majestically across the northern sky. Even Ron took time off for a quick look.

Soon we were over Holland and could see the flash of guns at the front near Arnhem, while on our starboard bow the blazing inferno of Duisburg, still being visited by the last of the Lancasters, could be seen. Searchlights were waving round it, while pinkish German fighter flares were still plopping down.

As planned, we passed close to the main bomber stream attack on Duisburg and then turned towards Münster (and then on to Hanover and Berlin our ultimate destination) with the intention of drawing off the night fighters from the main bomber stream. Heading towards Münster I saw that there were coloured flares at our altitude of 27,000 feet. These were not route marker flares for us, so I assumed that they were flares dropped by Germans to guide their night fighters. I altered the course towards Münster.

All was going well, we were perhaps two minutes from the turning point and Ron had just moved forward into the nose of the Mosquito to set up the bomb sight. He did this when we were around half an hour from reaching the target once he'd done some calculations based on the wind speeds that we were experiencing over Germany. Then at about 1.00 a.m. – flick! Two radar search-lights had us cold and naked in the smoky air. The amber 'boozer' light on the instrument panel illuminated brightly, indicating that the German radar for anti-aircraft guns or searchlights was locking on to us. I immediately altered course 30 degrees to starboard. More searchlights followed us until we shone like the fairy on the Christmas tree. Down I sank, focusing on the instruments inside the cabin, calling to Ron to keep his eyes skinned for anything as I couldn't look outside the plane myself for fear of temporarily losing my night vision in the glare of the searchlights. I then started our usual evasive action, beginning with a 30-degree turn to port and putting the nose down slightly to something like 195 knots (225 mph). Before I had counted much more than seventeen Ron said, 'Over to starboard now,' which rather surprised me but I took it to mean that he felt we were running directly over Münster and its anti-aircraft guns.

As we turned I had a glimpse of a row of pink night-fighter flares – about four – directly under-neath us and parallel to our track. 'German fighters,' I thought, then – click! I was blinded by a couple more searchlights that popped up behind the starboard engine. 'Blast,' I said. Then we must

5

have been hit, for the aircraft shook violently, and when my eyes once again became accustomed to the dull illumination of the instrument lights it was to see that we were climbing slightly. I went to ease the stick forward and it wouldn't move! With two hands I then shoved with all my might and the nose did pay off a little, but not enough. There was an awful feeling that we were climbing straight up. Then we snapped into a spin.

Down and down we went, seemingly flying straight down the searchlight beams, the aircraft screaming and juddering while bundles of the aluminium strips called Window floated up from the floor to land somewhere up in the roof. A huge 'G' force bore down on Ron and me. The normal drill of keeping my eyes focused on the instruments was impossible as the aircraft spun towards the searchlights.

Finally the rudder appeared to take effect and the spin slowed. After the glare of the searchlights the instrument panel was merely an orange blur to my dazzled vision. Then there was a world-ending crash with a simultaneous flick outwards of the fuselage – projecting me with tremendous force through the roof. A terrible, deadening roar beat on my eardrums and my immediate reaction was that I was having the king of all nightmares and that soon I would awake to find it a dream. But no! The aircraft seemed to have disintegrated and there I was, bowling end over end in space. Surely I had been strapped in my seat! Was my parachute still with me? Oh God, am I being killed?

I remembered my training in the United States,

which said that one should straighten one's legs to stop tumbling, so I did that and found that I fell more steadily. Now I could think about my parachute. I felt around to see if I was strapped in my seat and found that I was not, so I felt for the parachute ripcord. Sure enough there it was, and not a second after finding and pulling the ripcord there came the most satisfying 'whoof', followed by silence. I sensed drips of blood running down my face on to my Mae West. Perhaps the silence was only the contrast after the tremendous roaring and thundering as I left the plane; for soon, feeling a dull ache in both my arms, I looked upwards and saw the faint outline of the fat, round billowing canopy, and found my arms caught in the shroud lines above my head. Too weak at that altitude to move, I had to leave them there, but while beginning to take notice of these things I heard the quiet sighing of the wind in the shroud lines and canopy. Soon the ache in my arms became a pain and, after a struggle, I managed to free them, one at a time. But as I did so, I felt a fear that I might slip out of my harness. Then I started to swing rather badly. Eventually I was able to allay my fear of falling and stop the swinging at the same time, by the simple expedient of grasping the shroud lines on one side. When we went into that wall of searchlights at Münster I had seen a couple of Mosquitoes to the left and three to the right, so we were all quite close together. As I was falling through the air I was very conscious that there were other aircraft flying near by.

The searchlights were out now, but far above I

7

could still see a cluster of fighter flares, while in the distance below, two fires very close together were burning fiercely. My plane? Oh God! What about Ron? Please God, grant that he may have got out all right.

The great burden from this moment was what had happened to Ron. Ron normally sat alongside me, carrying out his navigation tasks with a plywood clipboard on his knee, except when he went forward into the nose of the plane to set the bomb sight. This had happened shortly before we were hit, which meant that Ron was without his parachute. Navigators only wore a harness and kept their parachute on the shelf next to their seat.

Down, down, down.

Below I began to make out a dark square, much blacker than the surrounding darkness. A forest! I'm coming down into a large forest – in Germany. What an adventure. Oh Ron! Please God help him. And while these thoughts were still running through my head – bump – I landed on my bottom in a ploughed field. This was my 'forest'; a newly ploughed field, not more than an acre or so. And a glance at my watch told me that my descent had taken me something like twenty minutes for it was just after 1.20 a.m.

Everything was deathly still and quiet. The wind was non-existent, so my chute collapsed with silken silence into a white half-moon upon the ground beside me. I listened. Nothing could be heard save the occasional distant bark of a dog and the faint rumble of aircraft engines high in the sky.

Chapter 2

Parents and Childhood

How did I come to be flying a Mosquito over Germany in the early hours of the morning of 15 October 1944?

My father, Henry Benifold Dell, joined the Royal Flying Corps (RFC) in early 1915 as he longed to fly. He had previously worked in the family furniture business and had been an enthusiastic cyclist and amateur car mechanic prior to the First World War. He assembled from bits three motor cars and would have preferred work that gave him an opportunity to use his mechanical skills. One of his proud boasts was that he had bought a car with a V4 engine, which had an irregular firing cycle, so he built a fifth cylinder, lengthening the crankshaft and camshaft and rearranging the timing.

Aged thirty-two when he enlisted, he was deemed to be too old to fly, but he was told that if he volunteered to work as a mechanic he might be able to get on to a flying course later. He spent 1915 and early 1916 at the airfield at St Omer in France, before being badly injured in a horrific accident that he was lucky to survive. In those days the procedure for starting an engine was for the mechanic, standing on the ground in front of the engine, to swing the propeller around for one revolution before telling the pilot to switch the engine on. Unfortunately a pilot had neglected to check that the switch was off before my father started this procedure and instead the engine immediately fired and the propeller began to revolve. My father was knocked to the ground and the rotating propeller hit his back and broke his arm. He was severely injured and had to be hospitalised and sent back to England to convalesce.

Once he had recovered my father was commissioned as an engineering officer, and put in a team of people brought together at the Central Flying School at Upavon. This team was dispatched to Canada in 1916 to set up flight training establishments for RFC pilots at Deseronto in Ontario. When the United States came into the war in April 1917 the flight training establishment was sent down to Fort Worth in Texas to train British and Canadian pilots.

While at Fort Worth my father got to know Vernon Castle, a pilot in the RFC who had fought on the Western Front and was the Chief Flying Instructor at Fort Worth. Prior to the war Castle and his American wife Irene were a famous pair of ballroom dancers, the world champions of the day, and responsible for popularising dances such as the foxtrot in the ragtime era. My father told me the story of watching Castle taking off with a pupil one day in 1918. The aircraft suffered an engine failure shortly after take-off and, in attempting to land, the aircraft clipped the top of a hanger and remained embedded in the roof before catching fire, both pilots burning to death before anyone could rescue them. A film *The Story of Vernon and*

Irene Castle (also known as *The Dancing Years*), starring Fred Astaire and Ginger Rogers as the Castles, with music by Irving Berlin, was made in 1939.

Father greatly enjoyed the male camaraderie in the RFC during the war, and when he returned to the United Kingdom at the end of the conflict he applied for a permanent commission in the newly established Royal Air Force (RAF). However, family interests prevailed and, even though he had a difficult relationship with his father, he agreed to work for him in the family furniture business.

My mother, Esme Duncan, was a very splendid person, utterly selfless, very much an idealist, with a strong religious side to her character. We always had prayers before bed and my mother went to the local Church of England church every Sunday morning. She was a fervent Conservative; she spent much of her life looking after the disadvantaged, but found socialism difficult, and was upset by the Labour victory in 1945. She had firm views on moral issues and was a strong advocate of equal rights for women; had circumstances been different she might have been a suffragette. She had a very good brain, wrote lovely poetry, and it was a sadness that she never went to university. My mother was head of the local branch of the Mothers' Union and much admired in our village. Many of the Mothers' Union ladies were widows from the First World War, and as a child I remember going along with my mother and a great fuss being made over me. Mother did her best to encourage me in the scholastic field,

11

and was a great communicator herself, writing me long letters when I was in the armed forces and away from home.

My parents got to know each other as very near neighbours when their families, the Dells and the Duncans, lived in large houses on the opposite side of a road in north Brighton. My father and mother married in 1910, my oldest brother Roger was born in 1911, my sister Betty in 1913, my brother John in 1919, and I was born in 1923. Roger went to sea in 1930 when I was seven and he was absent from home for most of my childhood. He became a ship's captain with the New Zealand Shipping Company. My sister Betty was also significantly older than me and after leaving education she went to secretarial school and then worked for two companies, one of which was Standard Oil, where she was assigned to the aviation department. During the Second World War she met a RAF officer and got married.

John was a Down's syndrome baby with severe behavioural difficulties which caused huge embarrassment for my family. When we went shopping, if he saw something that he particularly liked he would create a major fuss, and my mother, who had little enough money, would have to buy him something to get peace. In later life he had a job at a boat yard where the people were kind to him. He used to travel there by bus, and one day another passenger took offence at something that he'd done or said, so John was thrown off the bus by the conductor. From that day John developed an enmity towards conductors, bus drivers and the buses they drove – which unfortunately led him to hurl stones at buses as they went by. Every once in a while some member of the family had to make amends with the bus company because damage had been done. My father said that having John was like having a child at a boarding school for all your life because he was continually having to fork out money to meet poor John's unusual needs.

The bounds of social propriety were narrower in those days and behaviour that people would ignore or tolerate now was treated as a serious breach of social standards. My mother was very foresighted in trying to arrange John's life so that he could progress and live with the family when most Down's syndrome children in those days would have been shut away in an institution. A psychiatrist once commented that my mother was remarkable in the manner she had formulated a plan for John's life. She was a saint in the way she devoted her life to looking after him; she regarded him as her personal responsibility, and her great fear was that she might die before John.

My father was a very different character and I suspect that he had relationships outside the marital home, which had a bearing on my parents' marriage. At about the time that I first went to boarding school, when I was about eight years old, I remember being awakened in the night by a row between them. This troubled me greatly. I was probably closer to my father early on; later, as I realised how hard it was for my mother, with money short and the constant worries about John's future, I tended to be closer and more

13

sympathetic to her. I could see the burden that she was having to bear and felt that my father was not contributing as much support as he might have. There was very little I could do other than helping a little around the house, and it was very hard going off and not being around to support her, realising how tied she was to looking after John. I believe that the unhappiness in my parents' marriage could have resulted in divorce had it not been for the issue of how they would look after John if the marriage ended. Both my parents had a strong sense of duty, which they passed on to me as I grew up.

While mother went off to church on Sunday mornings my father would go down to Shoreham Harbour to work on the family boat. I usually went with him, except on Church high days like Christmas or Easter when I accompanied my mother. My father's activities in the RFC and his interest in sailing and sport (he played hockey) greatly appealed to me as a child. I learnt to do the sort of activities he did, and shared his regard for mechanical things. I had a strong interest in aircraft, which my father encouraged. He also supported my love of sport and I had an aptitude for most types of sport at school.

My father went to great lengths to involve me in the sort of things that he was engaged in, such as mechanical, boating and military matters. I can remember at the age of six or seven sitting on his lap as he read excerpts from Napoleon's campaigns to me. Together we would work out whether Napoleon and Wellington had played their cards right in the Peninsula Campaign and at Waterloo.

My grandfather had been an adventurous businessman with an eye for a bargain, and as a speculation he bought a farmhouse at a place called Upper Portslade, 6 miles from Brighton, with a surrounding 2½-acre meadow. This became our family home where I grew up as a child, and in many ways it gave me an idyllic childhood. I remember Christmas from the earliest age; all my mother's brothers and sisters would come down to the farmhouse from London. The farmhouse was great for family social occasions like this. The property had a lawn at the front of the house large enough for a tennis court, a barn, a dairy house, a small orchard and pasture. When I was very small my mother bought some chickens so we could have fresh eggs, and a little shed was built for the chickens to be kept in, with a hatchway to use to come and go. One of my first memories is as a toddler, squeezing through this little hole to get inside.

When I was about six years old I went to kindergarten and became friends with a boy called David Russell. David and I have remained pals ever since. We spent hours playing outside, climbing trees, playing games like cowboys and Indians, and trench warfare from the First World War. He and I built an aeroplane using my brother's tricycle as the undercarriage – in that respect rather ahead of its time. It consisted of two lengths of timber to which were nailed a tailplane and vertical rudder, with a crude propeller that could be turned with a crank handle, and a sheet scrounged from my mother to cover the wings. We hoisted this plane up into the lower branches of a big cedar tree and drew lots for the first flight. I won the privilege of command for the first flight and sat in the pilot's seat. David stood by with an axe and once I got the propeller turning fast David chopped the rope holding up the plane with his axe. The aeroplane fell straight down 10 feet and my brother's tricycle never ran straight again. David later became a parachutist and fought at Arnhem, so given the vertical trajectory of the plane perhaps this experience had some bearing on his choice of warfare!

Aviation had made a mark early on. We lived not far from Shoreham Airport and I would cycle over there with David and sit on the riverbank watching planes come and go, and in our imagination giving advice to the pilots on their technique. My father hadn't remained involved with flying but we were surrounded by relics of his wartime experiences in the RFC. The barometer in the house, which we used to tap to see what the weather was going to be like, was an altimeter from an aeroplane that he'd obtained during the war, and my mother grew geraniums in a pot that was the upturned cylinder from a plane's radial engine. My father retained his mechanical interests – he was always doing the maintenance of his own cars; when I was about eight I remember him taking off the cylinder head and helping him regrind the valves.

Times were very hard for small businesses in the Depression of the 1930s and the family furniture business struggled. My father told me that he was only able to run the business and pay the staff so long as the bank manager was prepared to keep increasing his overdraft. He managed to keep the business going and the staff employed, but money was a constant worry while I was a child. The housekeeping money for the week was produced for my mother on a Monday and it was sometimes difficult for my father to provide this. In later life it troubled me that money was such an embarrassment and I felt that he could have done more for my mother. As a child I very carefully saved up sixpences for a bicycle, and I remember that I was able to get a Hercules model on my birthday when a gift from my Aunt Mab – added to my savings and a contribution from my parents – met the purchase price of £3 18s 6d.

Money continued to be an issue for my family until 1936 when my father made contact with a big building firm and sold the old farmhouse and surrounding property for building development for a price of £10,000; a lot of money in those days. This sum enabled my father to pay off the bank overdraft and build a new house at Southwick, which was closer to Shoreham Harbour than the old farmhouse, and it became the family home for the next twenty years.

I enjoyed life at kindergarten but when I was eight years old I became a boarder at St Brides school in Hove. This was a very unhappy time because I was so conscious of the difficulties facing my mother and father. They sent me away, I think, believing that it would be better for me not to have all the trouble with John damaging me. In fact I understood very well what the problems were and would have preferred to be sharing

17

them rather than be away from the family. For this reason boarding was very stressful for me and I have always felt that children should not be separated from their parents in this way except in the most exceptional circumstances.

From St Brides I went to a prep school in Worthing from the age of ten or eleven, until I was thirteen. I was very keen on sport and was always in the first team, playing soccer in winter, rugby in spring and cricket in summer. I tolerated the academic side of school life, but was far from being a dedicated scholar.

It was galling to be at boarding school, cut off from all the interesting and important things that I could do at home, like making things, having adventures, and sailing dinghies. Holidays were a welcome respite from the tedium of school. David and I built a canoe that we used to go paddling in within Shoreham Harbour. Boarding school seemed very limited and boring in comparison; outside the classroom I did a lot of reading, played sports such as fives, and used to make model planes, but I really looked forward to returning home for the holidays.

My father used to say that a branch of the family in an earlier era had run a fleet of fishing boats in the River Thames and that water ran in our blood. Before the First World War he had some sort of small boat and after the war he came upon the hull of quite a big yacht 30 or 40 feet long. The lead keel of the yacht had been cut off during the war when the value of this metal reached an astronomical level, so my father hauled the boat up, built a wooden mould under it, and cast a concrete keel in the place that was previously occupied by the lead one. Of course the specific gravity of concrete is very different to lead and the only way we could keep the boat upright was to put pig iron under the floor as ballast. I spent a lot of time working with my father, maintaining the yacht and learning to sail – this experience came in handy when I learnt to fly. Our summer holiday invariably followed a pattern of sailing the boat westwards for two to three weeks, usually towards Dartmouth. My mother would have enjoyed staying in a hotel for a break from cooking and housework, but because of my brother John that would have been an embarrassment for her, while going on the boat with John and me was fine.

I was initially quite slow in learning to read. What eventually gave me the motivation was the wish to read newspapers. My family always got the *Daily Mail*, which at that time always had photos on the front of the great things that were happening around the world, and I wanted to read it to know the background to these photos. I became an avid reader of newspapers and very aware of what was going on. I read about the launching of the *Queen Mary* in 1934 (I can still recall that its number on the slip was 534), and about the completion of the Sydney Harbour Bridge in 1932. In retrospect, events like these indicated that the Depression was slowly coming to an end. I remember reading of great parades in Germany and seeing pictures of a chap called Hitler. The 'Bodyline' test series in Australia made a great impact; it didn't seem quite right to me to be aiming for the man not the stumps.

19

Once I had mastered the art I was a voracious reader, enjoying such titles as T.E. Lawrence's *Seven Pillars of Wisdom* when I was thirteen or so, and books by R.L. Stevenson and John Masefield. Then there was Robert Graves's *Goodbye To All That* and later Ernest Hemingway's *For Whom the Bell Tolls*. Aviation magazines such as *Flight* and *The Aeroplane* were seldom missed when they came out each month.

Mother would only take us to the cinema on rainy days; when the sun was shining we were expected to be outside playing. I saw *The Charge of the Light Brigade, Dawn Patrol,* the movies of Laurel and Hardy, and the early Walt Disney films. There was always a newsreel, British Movietone news, and at the bigger cinemas there was a cinema organ. My family were relatively late getting a radio; my father bought our first radio in the late 1930s, and after that we regularly listened to the six o'clock news.

The everyday encounters with the consequences of the Depression made a strong impression on one growing up in the 1930s. Once, someone reported to my mother that there was a local family in the village in difficult circumstances and she took me to their house with a large loaf of bread and a bowl of beef dripping, knowing that they had no food. Week by week men would knock at our door asking for work of any type, offering to charge just half a crown to mow the lawn or do odd jobs around the house. Many of them were ex-servicemen, wearing their tunics from the First World War to show that they had done their bit. Although I was just a small boy I asked my father why we were in this state and I remember him saying, 'Too much buying on the never-never.' In 1932 the country was virtually bankrupt and could no longer pay the Americans interest on our war loan and this precipitated the worst phase of the Depression.

At the time of King Edward's abdication in 1936, the whole school was summoned to the assembly hall where a radio was put up on the stage and we heard his abdication speech. It was a bizarre happening and in the *Daily Mail* one saw pictures of Edward and Mrs Simpson on a yacht called the *Nahlin* cruising around the Mediterranean, so we were aware of this divorcee who was having her way with our King. Mother felt that the right thing was done in the end; she did not approve of Mrs Simpson and thought her well beyond the pale. George VI came to the throne and at the time we were very conscious of his speech impediment. I remember listening to one of his Christmas Day speeches on the radio and noticing that he kept hesitating as he spoke.

The experience of the First World War was very present in day-to-day life; there were so many unmarried aunts because of the loss of men during the war, and there was still an air of great sadness across the country. Just outside Brighton, at Roedean, there was a huge military hospital full of soldiers, most of whom had been blinded by mustard gas in the war. Armistice Day was a very important day; my father would put on his medals, we would usually go to church, then the family would go to the local war memorial. In 1937 my parents sent my sister Betty and I on a tour of Belgium. We spent ten days being taken around by motor coaches to see the sights, in particular the battlefields of the First World War, including the vast cemeteries. This made a great impression on me; I recall saying to my sister, 'This can never happen again, it's far too terrible.' A strong pacifist feeling was common but there was also a strong body of public opinion that felt that we should be confronting some of the dangers we were facing. The name of Churchill was bandied about as someone who stood for this.

My parents paid for another holiday for my sister and myself in Brittany in France, which coincided with the Munich crisis in September 1938 when Germany threatened to go to war with Britain and France over its territorial claims in Czechoslovakia. After crossing to St Malo by ferry, we travelled by rail and saw trains full of French sailors who were being mobilised and going to rejoin their ships in Brest and St Nazaire. I can't recall whether the sailors were particularly enthusiastic or sombre but there was a feeling of some relief in England when Chamberlain came back from Munich waving his famous piece of paper signed by Hitler. War was avoided for the time being, giving us some breathing space to strengthen the RAF and other armed forces. To me it seemed a climb-down and I wasn't impressed with Chamberlain's leadership. This appeared to be the general view once the immediate feeling of relief had passed.

In 1937 at the end of prep school I won a scholarship to Dover College, a public school founded in the nineteenth century on the site of a medieval priory. I think that I got the scholarship with basic intelligence and low cunning rather than scholastic achievement. Dover College was a good school, although I always felt that it was pretending to be something it was really not: an imitation of its closest competitor Kings School in Canterbury, an old established institution. I did tolerably well at Dover College, playing for the first teams for cricket and rugby, and other sports that involved balls, like squash, fives and tennis.

When war broke out in September 1939 I was still at school and considering what I would do when I left. Of course, I could have gone into my father's furniture business, but the unhappiness of the Depression still hung over it, with its over-stretched finances. I was more interested in joining the Royal Air Force or becoming a civil engineer. One of the attractions of joining the Air Force was the opportunity for sport, which I knew I was good at, but was I capable enough for a place at Cranwell, the RAF's training and education academy?

What sort of a young man was I then? I was confident of my ability in sport, which meant a lot at that age in a public school environment. The influence of my mother meant that I had a strong sense of responsibility. My friends and I thought that we were worldly and sophisticated, and certainly I do not believe that we were as wide-eyed and naïve as the 1914 generation appear to have been. We grew up with the shadow of the First World War and the Depression and the likelihood that another war was imminent. Nonetheless, I don't think that any of us were particularly downcast; the natural exuberance of youth prevailed.

Chapter 3

The Outbreak of War

The announcement of the pact between Germany and Russia in August 1939 left a strong impression and the subsequent invasion of Poland was no great surprise. Neville Chamberlain's speech announcing Britain's declaration of war occurred on a Sunday morning and we had been alerted in advance to the speech. I sat in our living room at home with the rest of the family, listening on the radio. The speech itself was uninspired. Immediately after it ended all the air-raid alarms sounded, and we all went to the study – which we thought was the safest room in the house – to await the German bombers that we expected to be overhead. The view at the time was 'the bomber will always get through' as the former Prime Minister Stanley Baldwin had said. We had already taken the precaution of putting tape over the windows to reduce the risk from flying glass caused by bombing. Based on the experience from the First World War we thought that the Germans might also try using poison gas, so we had our gas masks with us. Nothing happened – there were no German bombers overhead – and the 'all clear' sounded shortly afterwards.

My friends and family all felt apprehensive about the war. After the awfulness of the First World War no one had any illusions about a quick or easy war; we fully realised the seriousness of what we were facing. Britain had a powerful Navy but it was common knowledge that the Germans had a marked superiority in their army and air force, so the prospects did not look particularly good.

There was a widespread feeling of anticlimax over the next few months during the 'phoney war' period. The scuttling of the *Graf Spee* after the Battle of the River Plate was one of the few significant events over the first winter of the war and got great publicity. I didn't go to the cinema while at boarding school; instead we all read the newspapers, which were laid out for us each morning.

Dover College had been evacuated during the First World War and it was recognised that we could be in range of guns on the French coast if the Germans successfully invaded France. So the school was evacuated to Tiverton in Devon, where we shared classes and grounds with another school, Blundell's. This was an unsettled period. I was endeavouring to work on science subjects at Dover College, but in Devon we didn't have the use of laboratories so I was summoned to discuss the issue of a replacement subject with the headmaster. He tried to persuade me to take Latin but I said to him that I couldn't see that Latin was going to be of any great use to me in the future and that I preferred not to do it. He said, 'All right I'll put you down for geography.' This proved to be invaluable.

At school I reached the Fifth form rather than joining the true scholars in the Sixth form and I continued to do well at sport. If I could see the point of an objective I could make an effort and I got quite good reports in subjects that appealed to me.

The rapid fall of France in May 1940 came as a terrible shock. The evacuation from Dunkirk coincided with the end of the Easter holidays and, as I returned to school, the train to Tiverton was full of soldiers evacuated from the fighting in France. They looked in a bad way. The word went around that anyone with a serviceable boat could help with the evacuation and my father thought seriously about taking his yacht to Dunkirk, but it had already been laid up in a berth at Southwick for the winter. With its deep keel, the yacht would not have been ideal for getting close into shore to take soldiers off the shallow beach anyway. Winston Churchill became Prime Minister at this time and tried to portray Dunkirk as a victory in defeat, which we all saw through, although it was a great achievement at least in getting the soldiers off the beaches. People had a great admiration for Churchill as a personality; he was a real leader of men and made a fine impression with the stirring speeches that he made at the time. Even as a schoolboy I was very pleased to see him take over from Chamberlain.

The Battle of Britain was being fought overhead when I came home from school for the summer break in 1940. One day I watched a German Me110 flying low across the village and firing its machine guns – I found out later that our local butcher's delivery boy was killed by this plane while riding his bike across our village green with his packages. A few days later a German Heinkel dropped a string of bombs in Kingston Lane, not far from our house. A dear old lady was killed in her kitchen. Other bombs put a hole in the quayside not far from my father's boat, which was left covered in debris. I thought that this was absolutely terrible, although it was insignificant compared to the damage that the Luftwaffe inflicted on London and cities like Coventry later in the war. How dare they do this! As a legacy of the First World War I had grown up always regarding the Germans as the enemy, and they were always so in children's games. The friendly feelings towards Germany that were held in some parts of society between the wars weren't shared by people that I knew.

At home we were well placed to see the dogfights between planes during the Battle of Britain. One day I was standing in our garden with my father, and we watched a Spitfire hit in a dogfight at a great height come down in a steep dive. We both shouted, 'Pull out, pull out', but the Spitfire continued in its dive and hit the ground a couple of miles away in Hove. During the Battle there were optimistic newspaper headlines claiming high enemy losses, but we did not feel confident that we were necessarily winning; it seemed a hard fight and victory looked to be a long way away. We were very conscious that only

27

600 British fighters were facing a German force of 2,400 aircraft.

When at home in the daytime my father used to put a ladder up against the side of our house and go up to the roof, which was a V shape, to get a better view of the fighting in the air above. Once while he was up there a German Heinkel came over very low, pursued by two Hurricanes firing their machine guns at it. My father was unharmed, but this experience scared the living daylights out of him, and he never went up to the roof again.

My family were very patriotic. There was never any doubt that I would join up as soon as I was able and this attitude was shared by all my school friends – it was simply the thing to do. During the First World War my mother had soldiers billeted with her at the old farmhouse at Upper Portslade. She used to listen to their stories and related them to us as children. I grew up hearing these tales about the Western Front, and seeing at school the list of 250 or so former Dover College pupils who had been killed, so my friends and I were under no illusions about the nature of war and the terrible human consequences. We believed that war was necessary where the cause was just.

Chapter 4

The Home Guard

In May 1940, before the battle for France had concluded, notices were put in the newspapers and announcements made on the radio inviting all men between sixteen and sixty to join the Local Defence Volunteers (renamed as the Home Guard in July 1940). I was in the Officer Training Corps at my public school so I was already familiar with drill and handling guns. I put my name down when I returned home for the summer holidays, was accepted, and two to three evenings a week I would report to the local Home Guard HQ. There we would have drills and be lectured on the use of weapons and how we might be deployed.

The great fear of the time was the threat of German parachutists being dropped inland to seize the ports from behind, to enable the main invading force to disembark, as the Germans only had canal barges that were unsuitable for beaching and required ports with wharves. My Home Guard unit was required to dig trenches on top of the South Downs in case we had to make a stand against the parachutists. We also had lectures in unarmed combat from members of the Home Guard who had recently fought in the Spanish Civil War. I remember learning how to strangle an enemy sentry, how to stick a hat pin through his throat so that he couldn't shout, and where to jab a knife into him, and useful things like that – dear oh dear! Despite this bloodthirsty training there was no great apprehension in the unit; the feeling was always light-hearted and we were optimistic that it would turn out all right, although one simply could not see how this would be.

My unit comprised a number of veterans from the First World War, and a mix of older men and young men like myself. It was my first experience of being treated as an adult, but I took it in my stride; the dirty stories told by some of the men were merely an extension of public school life – we considered ourselves men of the world! The unit included one or two spivs, who would turn up on parade and ask, 'Anyone want any nylon stockings, a bottle of whisky?' – exactly like Private Walker in *Dad's Army*. Eventually one of the spivs was called up to serve in the regular Army and there was all sorts of hue and cry as, predictably, his kit and various items of military equipment disappeared with him.

In *Dad's Army* Captain Mainwaring's unit drove around in a butcher's van; in our unit we used to travel in a coalman's truck. Our company commander, Lieutenant Pinnel, was the local newsagent, a veteran from the First World War, and like Captain Mainwaring a little pompous. There was one episode when after an exercise on the Downs we were marching back to base; when passing a local pub, all of the unit peeled off to have a drink without any order to fall out, leaving our commander fuming. Based on my own experience there was relatively little exaggeration in the portrayal of the Home Guard in *Dad's Army* and there was plenty of comic potential with my comrades – and a touch of the hapless Private Pike in myself. While the Home Guard had a serious purpose, by and large it was fun for a schoolboy like myself.

In every unit in the British Army there is always a humorist. We had a chap of about sixty called Saxby who'd been a bosun at sea, knew the seamy side of life, and had a constant fund of vulgar stories. He was now working as a church verger and digging the graves in the church's cemetery. After I went back to school I heard from a colleague in our unit that one day our unit was to be addressed by the regular Army general who commanded the forces on the coast, one Bernard Montgomery, who was unknown to the public at the time but went on to greater things as the war progressed. Saxby was firmly instructed beforehand: 'Now Saxby you're not to tell any of your stories during the parade and if the general stands in front of you don't say a word to him.' Inevitably Montgomery paused in front of Saxby in the course of his inspection and asked some questions. Saxby followed his orders to the letter and didn't make any reply, instead maintaining a most uncharacteristic silence in the face of the questioning – which must have left Montgomery nonplussed. In his speech to the unit Montgomery made the sensible point that they should keep their bicycles handy so that if German parachutists did land they could get to attack them as quickly as possible.

From time to time we would join up with neighbouring units for exercises. One evening we went inland near a village called Steyning, where we were taken to a chalk pit, issued with hand grenades, and taught how to throw them. Each one of us was allowed to lob a single live hand grenade as practice. We were not told at the time but I later found out that the chalk pit contained drums of mustard gas, which would be used against the Germans in the event of an invasion. Clearly the Government had decided to take the gloves off if the Germans invaded and anything possible would have been used to stop them coming ashore, including dropping petrol on the sea and setting it alight. In one corner of the pit there was an enormous howitzer capable of firing 10-inch naval shells on to any beach between Newhaven and Worthing should the invasion take place. Little did the world know of these goings-on.

Another day of training for my unit involved the use of a small cannon, which looked as though it had been made in someone's home workshop. The cannon had a barrel about 6 feet long and it was mounted on a crude chassis so that it could be wheeled around. The projectiles looked like – and may in fact have been – Coca-Cola bottles. The cannon was loaded by opening a crude breech block at the back, the Coca-Cola bottle was placed in with a white linen bag of gunpowder, the breech was slammed shut, and the gun fired by putting in a blank .22 cartridge in a touchhole with some sort of striking mechanism.

The bottles contained phosphorous and were intended to be fired against tanks, the idea being that the phosphorous would burn like crazy and incinerate the people inside the tank. I saw the cannon fired once. The company commander said, 'Let's try two Coca-Cola bottles'; this was duly done and a gigantic flame came from the muzzle of the gun. The result looked spectacular, although I doubt that it would have been an effective weapon against any German Panzer.

A neighbouring unit showed off a German flamethrower captured in the First World War, retrieved from a military museum and pressed into service. This had a big tank that was to be filled with paraffin and creosote, and connected to a high-pressure system with compressed air and thence a hosepipe to a burner. I never saw it in action but it was installed at a bend in the road so that any German vehicle that came around it could be attacked.

On one night – I think the night of 15 August at the height of the Battle of Britain – my unit was ordered to stand-to and sent up to the trenches we had dug on top of the South Downs, as there was an expectation that the invasion might take place that night. Looking northwards in the direction of London one could see the whole sky illuminated from fires from German air raids on south London; apparently a number of factories around Croydon were hit. There was a huge glowing light to the east, and in our excited state we assumed that it was Brighton in flames. Shortly afterwards the moon came up and we realised that there was a more innocent explanation for the glow. The sergeant came around and issued us each with ten rounds of ammunition for the American rifles from the 1914 to 1918 war that my unit was armed with. We said to him, 'Once we've used our ten rounds is this all we have?', and he replied that he was keeping another ten rounds for each of us in reserve. So we were going into battle with a maximum of twenty rounds each! It was a great relief that nothing eventuated. I dread to think of the consequences if we had ever found ourselves trying to fight off a German invasion. We were all very determined and I'm sure we would have fought resolutely, but we were so poorly equipped that I'm sure the outcome in a fight with professionally trained and equipped soldiers would have been an unequal mismatch.

On another night we were guarding a path that went to a lock on a canal and a power station. We had been instructed that if we saw yellow rockets out to sea this meant that enemy shipping had been sighted and we should report it to Home Guard HQ. If red rockets were sighted, the German invasion was definitely happening. Not long after we took up our positions we saw yellow rockets out to sea so I was dispatched to the nearest telephone box to relate this news to HQ, as it might be the precursor to a full invasion assault. To my embarrassment I didn't have any money on me so I had to ask the woman operator if HQ would accept the charges for a collect call. There was silence as the operator rang through to HQ and asked them to accept my call. Then, to my consternation, she came back to me and said that HQ would not accept a collect call. I felt very conscious of the serious responsibility placed on me and I became greatly alarmed and insisted that she try again.

I persisted and eventually HQ were persuaded to accept the call. I reported the yellow rockets to the Company Commander who said, 'Well there's nothing that I can do about it', and just told me to go back to my post. Fortunately for everyone there were no red rockets that night, or any other night. Years later I met Clement Attlee, who was Deputy Prime Minister at this time, and told him about my rather farcical experiences defending England from German invasion in 1940. He did not seem particularly impressed. Not even a smile.

After the summer holidays ended in September 1940, I went back to school for a final autumn term. I had taken the Oxford and Cambridge Joint Board School Certificates exam before the summer break and did reasonably well overall, but got bad marks in maths and decided to return for the autumn term to resit the exam. In the event I passed six subjects with credit; this was the equivalent of Matric, and if you had Matric you were qualified for university entrance, which was my immediate goal.

At school I retained a Browning automatic rifle that I had been issued with in the Home Guard and created a bit of a stir by leaving it propped up at the end of my bed. The Officer Training Corps (OTC) at school had exercises with the local Home Guard at Tiverton and I gave the Home Guard instruction in how to use the Browning automatic rifle, although I think the First World War veterans in the Home Guard soon surpassed the proficiency of their seventeen-year-old instructor. The OTC had the status of a Home Guard unit and we took turns acting as sentries every night, guarding the school and looking out for German parachutists.

Chapter 5

The Royal Air Force and Training in the United States

In late 1940, in the middle of the London Blitz while the outcome of the air attack on Britain was still far from clear, the newspapers had advertised a year-long university short course in science offered by the RAF, with the understanding that the full degree could be completed after the war and could lead to a long-term RAF career. This seemed a rather optimistic undertaking, given the grim situation in the war at the time, but I successfully applied and was allocated to a course at Aberdeen University. I travelled up to Aberdeen where I was enrolled in the Air Training Corps, issued with a uniform, did some drill (I didn't have to do an Initial Training Wing (ITW) course as the university course was viewed as equating to ITW) and then commenced training.

Aberdeen struck me as a distinguished city, but rather austere; all the buildings were grey, with slate roofs and stone walls, and the climate was not benign. North of the city was a fine sandy beach, but we found that swimming even in mid-summer was like jumping on to an iceberg. I was immensely proud to have got into the RAF. So soon after the Battle of Britain, airmen stood high in the public estimation, although we were disappointed to find that girls were not especially impressed by the status of air cadets who had not yet earned their wings. The group of thirty or so other students on the course were a convivial gang, all enthusiastic and itching to fly. We quickly established friendships. My particular friend was Victor Crauford, who came from a farming family in Lincolnshire. Like others on the course we shared digs with two middle-aged ladies at their house at 169 Great Western Road. They gave us breakfast each morning and 'high tea' each evening. Once in a while salmon would be served with a wink and a whispered ''Tis poached don't ye know', which did not refer to the mode of cooking. They had a brother with unorthodox and varied skills.

I found I fitted into the RAF culture easily, the discipline was more relaxed than in the Army (or for that matter the United States Army Air Force (USAAF)) and in many respects it was a natural extension of my public school, except with a greater mixture of social classes. One of my best friends in the RAF, John Metcalfe, had delivered coal before the war, and I think that the RAF was a genuine meritocracy. We were judged by our individual competency and effectiveness and I think that this was reflected in the RAF's achievements during the war.

There was a great deal of inter-service rivalry between Army, Navy and Air Force, which showed itself in disparaging comments when we met with friends in the different branches of the armed services. We used to say: 'In the Air Force we have wine, women and song; in the Navy they have rum, bum and gramophone records.' My RAF colleagues and I viewed the Army officer corps as bumbling aristocrats, and my dear friend David Russell, who chose to join the Army, was very conscious of the class divisions that persisted in some parts of it, particularly in the Guards regiments. In the RAF we felt that the Navy lived on tradition to an unhealthy degree and the sailors I met appeared slow to appreciate the vulnerability of their ships to air attack. During my training I was warned never to fly over British shipping as they would loose off every antiaircraft gun they had against overhead aircraft, friendly or hostile.

Our scholastic subjects were taught for the most part at King's College a little way out of town; our RAF subjects and our cadet activities were conducted at Marischal College at the bottom of the main street. The latter was the chief administration building of the university, the location of the Students' Union and dining room, and very much the centre of university life. It also had a fine gymnasium, long remembered by me because this is where I lost my two front teeth after a bad landing over the vaulting horse.

In our limited spare time Victor and I took part in the university sporting life, both of us representing the institution against St Andrews in athletics. There was great emphasis on sport of every sort in the RAF (again in contrast to the USAAF) and every station had rugby and cricket teams, and many had facilities like squash courts. We even went to dancing classes together, hoping that this might pull the birds in later life. Victor was better than I in both cases. He was a good-hearted, open and athletic schoolboy. After training in the United States Victor returned to the UK and became a Lancaster pilot in 1943, the very worst time to be in Bomber Command. His aircraft crashed in Holland returning from a raid and he was killed. I subsequently spent a sad day with his father at their farm; he was very kind to me despite his loss.

Once in a while students on the course were taken out to the RAF base at Dyce near Aberdeen and we all had at least one flight in an operational aircraft over the North Sea. This was my first flight ever, on a Bristol Blenheim, an aircraft that had been originally designed as a light pre-war bomber and later modified to operate as a fighter, although it was outclassed by 1941. I found my first flight an exhilarating experience. After we landed and taxied to the parking place I was the first to disembark, then, as one of my friends got out, the ripcord handle of his parachute caught on something, the parachute burst open, and the cockpit filled with silk and cordage. The squadron CO, who had piloted the flight, was furious and gave my friend a blast for being so careless. However, when the CO himself undid his safety harness and eased himself out of his seat, he inadvertently pushed the machine-gun fire button and the plane's five machine guns fired a burst, sending bullets across the airfield and leaving a small pyramid of spent cartridges underneath each gun. He was most shamefaced and it was very fortunate that no one had been hit by the bullets.

On RAF cadet days we wore our training corps uniforms, with silver buttons as opposed to brass, took part in drilling on a parade ground and attended lectures on aeronautical subjects such as Navigation, Meteorology, Theory of Flight, Morse Code and Radio and so forth. I found the academic side of the course quite hard going. During our lectures on meteorology, one day a professor took us up one of the towers of King's College to point out the features of the clouds overhead. From the tower we saw a plane doing a couple of leisurely circuits over the port below and we students confidently assured the professor that the plane was a Blenheim from the Dyce air base. After two circuits the 'Blenheim' dropped a string of bombs on the port and then raced off towards the North Sea – it was actually a German Junkers Ju88 bomber.

My first year course in Aberdeen lasted nine months, with only a fortnight break at home in the summer. When it finished in October 1941 we were sent to the Air Crew Reception Centre in London, where we were billeted in empty apartments around Regent's Park. While here we took meals in the cafeteria of London Zoo, were issued with uniforms at Lord's Cricket Ground, and received medical inspections and antitetanus injections. For the first time I felt that I was really in the RAF and received my first pay. After two weeks a group of fifty of us were sent to an airfield called Booker near Marlow, where there was a Grading School with Tiger Moth aircraft. Here we were given ten hours of basic flying instruction in order to determine whether we really had the makings to be pilots – there being no point in shipping us overseas for full training if we didn't. I had always wanted to fly, and felt immediately that I had the aptitude. In many respects flying had a similarity to sailing a dinghy, with which I had plenty of experience. At this stage I was only eighteen years old and did not have a driving licence.

In Tiger Moths the instructor and trainee sat one behind the other with a Gosport Tube between them so they could communicate by shouting down the tube. After a maximum of ten hours' dual control flying we were expected to be at a point where we were ready to go solo, from which point we would continue with our training overseas. Apparently I was able to persuade my instructor that I was ready to go solo after a good deal less than ten hours.

My mother said I had a weak chest as a boy, and towards the end of the course at Booker I developed bronchitis, and was put in the station hospital for a couple of weeks. This meant that I was not able to go overseas with the friends I'd been with for almost a year, and instead had to wait for the next batch. I had always had the ambition to pilot flying boats, and to my chagrin the rest of my original group of trainees were sent to the US Navy base at Pensacola to learn on Catalina flying boats. Missing out on this was a huge disappointment. One of my friends, David Owen, completed the course and then got a role ferrying flying boats between the United States and Britain. This seemed a relatively safe job, but on a return trip the Liberator that David was travelling on as a passenger flew into a mountain and he was killed.

Before I left for the United States I stayed with my family at Southwick and took the opportunity to visit my sister Betty who was living in London in a flat near Victoria Station. The railway line into Victoria passed close by rows of buildings four storeys high; during 1940 many of these had been blown away by bombs. I noticed that on one there were the remnants of a fourth-floor wall, with a suit hanging on a coat hanger amid the ruins. I'd look out for this suit each time I passed by in the train and it was there for some years. I also remember a Heinkel bomber that had crashed on the roof of Victoria Station and it remained there for quite a while.

It was already dark when I arrived to visit Betty and I stumbled around in the blackout until I found the front door of her house and pushed the bell. There was no response; then stepping back from the door I saw the moon through the stained-glass windowpane and realised that the back of the house I was trying to enter had been blown off by a bomb blast. I was horrified and had a bad moment before I discovered that I was at the wrong address. I found the right address with Betty's flat still intact just down the road.

As has often been observed, there was a unique sense of unity and purpose apparent in England at this time. Social barriers broke down and people would talk to one another in unusual circumstances in a most un-English way. When visiting London a high percentage of people were in uniforms and the sheer variety of different uniforms was remarkable, not just the British Army, Navy and Air Force, but the uniforms of various colonial units and of the different Occupied countries – the Free French, Polish, Czechs, Belgians, Dutch and other nations. The blackout made travelling after dark difficult, and in London one was always on the alert for air raids, but many aspects of life went on as they had in pre-war days. I never had much money so tended not to take girls to cinemas or live music. The great thing for me and my friends was to go to the pub, where we played pub games like darts, dominoes and shove-halfpenny. American culture was a strong influence and it was the era of big bands like Glenn Miller, Tommy Dorsey, Artie Shaw and Duke Ellington. On the radio the weekly highlight was *It's That Man Again* (ITMA) with Tommy Handley on a Thursday night.

I finally left for training overseas with the next group of trainees at the end of December 1941, boarding the *Montcalm,* a 16,000-tonne Canadian Pacific liner, in Liverpool on New Year's Eve. Previously airmen travelling to the United States for training had worn civilian clothes in recognition of American neutrality, but as this was shortly after Pearl Harbor we were all in uniform. I was greatly relieved that the Americans had joined us at long last and thought that the Japanese had done us a favour by overcoming the American opposition to Roosevelt's wish to join the war. I had been astonished that the Germans had invaded Russia and that we were now also allies with Stalin. The Russians seemed an unlikely ally as, prior to the war, there had been headlines in the papers about Gulags in Russia where political prisoners were sent, and it was common knowledge that many of the Russian High Command had been executed in Stalin's purges.

The weather at sea was terrible and the crossing to Halifax in Canada took fourteen days. We were not travelling in convoy and went quite far down south in the Atlantic to avoid submarines. We were escorted by a First World War American Navy destroyer, which had a Royal Navy crew, and in rough seas the destroyer was rolling so heavily that from our ship we could see down its funnels. I was used to boats and seafaring but had never experienced conditions as awful and miserable as this and I became very seasick like so many others aboard. At least I felt vindicated in choosing a career with the RAF over one in the Royal Navy.

On the deck of the *Montcalm* there was a hydrovane – a device that looked like a torpedo with wings, which could be towed at an angle beside the ship on a towline, like a kite in the water – used to chop mines off their moorings. In the very heavy weather every second or third wave crashed over the deck causing the hydrovane to tear itself from its attachments and smash backwards and forwards, doing great damage. A group of us were in a cabin in the forecastle in the bows of the ship when the hydrovane started to loosen the deck plates above us, making a tremendous noise and causing water to leak into the cabin. We ended up with six inches of water sloshing back and forth on the floor of the cabin, with objects like gas masks and socks floating on top.

We were very relieved and absolutely starving when we finally arrived at the port of Halifax. I went around three times at the buffet for the first breakfast that I had on dry land. From Halifax we were sent to the nearby depot at Moncton for three weeks before leaving on a three-day train journey to Turner Field, a USAAF airbase at Albany, Georgia. Here we were issued with American uniforms and spent a few weeks being indoctrinated into life in the USAAF, learning American drill and discipline. Based on West Point standards, discipline seemed very strict in comparison to the free and easy life in the RAF one had been used to. Demerit points were the order of the day for quite minor infringements of the rules. If a certain limit was passed one was thrown off the course so they were no laughing matter. Even crossing the road had to be done at right angles. One night two or three of the American officers in charge of us marched into our barracks and called a parade. We were in our pyjamas and they berated us for not having immediately stood up when they came in, and required us to parade outside in the cold, dressed as we were. This led to quite a bit of friction early on between the British airmen and our American hosts.

I was one of three on my course picked out to be cadet officers, each with around 100 people under our command when we paraded. Every morning we paraded and were meant to march to and fro past our barracks. On one occasion all of the aircrew suddenly decided as a lark on an early return to barracks, leaving me embarrassed and plaintively asking them if they would be so kind as to continue marching. I had to plead with them to return amid much hilarity. I survived!

While at Turner Field I again went down with bronchitis and spent a couple of weeks recovering in a military hospital. In an adjacent bed was an American sailor suffering from burns experienced in the Japanese surprise raid on Pearl Harbor. He told me about his experiences in the devastating attack but obviously he and all the other survivors had been briefed not to disclose details of all the ships sunk.

Overall, my impressions of the United States were very positive. The weather was fine and warm after the grey of an English winter, people were very friendly in the small southern towns where air bases were located, and it was nice meeting so many young people. There was an extraordinary contrast between the youthful enthusiastic spirit in the United States and the grim struggle going on in Europe. I was very impressed by how hard everyone worked, the businesslike way they went about things and the American ability to organise on a huge scale. I greatly enjoyed my time there. I didn't feel guilty about being in the United States at this time as I always knew that I was going back to England to face the music, but I felt sorry for the folks back home with the blackout, rationing and the tough wartime conditions that they had to put up with while we enjoyed the good things of life.

One of the few troubling aspects of living in the United States was the attitude towards Negroes in the southern states. I remember one incident where I went to sit at the back of a bus, not knowing that this section of the bus was reserved for Negroes to sit. Disapproving looks from white passengers told the story. I was very uncomfortable with the attitude of white Americans towards Negroes; it was contrary to my own beliefs and the way that I had been brought up. Later on while I was instructing there was a black man who looked after our block of accommodation; we got talking one day and I asked him how much he was paid – it turned out to be the same as me! Regrettably this was primarily a reflection of the poor pay rates in the British armed forces rather than any racially enlightened pay policy in the United States. He could afford to run an old car, which I could not do while at the same time meeting my Mess bill each month.

After Albany, my training group was divided up and sent to primary flying schools around the southern states. I was sent to Tuscaloosa, Alabama, where I learnt to fly the Boeing-Stearman Model 75. This was a biplane trainer, equivalent to the Tiger Moth that I had flown in England, but far superior, with a big powerful radial engine, wheels with brakes, and a steerable tail wheel. It flew beautifully and I took to it at once. With its open cockpit, it gave one a marvellous feeling of freedom, and it was fantastic flying such a responsive plane. Of course, there was considerable tension as one approached flying solo for the first time, but once I'd done it I felt I was king of the castle.

Interestingly, it was the US Air Corps' philosophy at the time that one should learn to fly 'by the seat of your pants' as the saying went, with little reliance on flying instruments, unlike the RAF, which insisted on the latter from the very beginning. Instrument flying was left to the next phase of training, referred to as Basic. This resulted in the rear cockpits, where the trainee sat, being equipped with minimum instrumentation. Once flying, the braver souls (including myself on one occasion) would sometimes unstrap, stand up and peer into the empty front cockpit to check how fast they were going, as measured by the airspeed indicator. Which philosophy was superior is debatable, but one certainly graduated with a feeling of confidence in the man and machine interaction.

The instructors who taught us at Tuscaloosa were civilians, some of whom had learnt to fly during the First World War. All were characters, well chosen, and some with interesting tales to tell. One or two had flown liquor from Canada to the United States during Prohibition. One man had been in the German Luftwaffe! My own instructor shared ownership of a Fokker Trimotor (the same type of plane as Charles Kingsford-Smith's famous *Southern Cross*) and had a business offering joyrides to the public, particularly at air shows. Barnstorming he called it. A good steady man.

I was at Tuscaloosa for six weeks. Tuscaloosa happened to be the location of the University of Alabama and one of the colleges, an all-women's college, invited some of the air cadets to a dance. We were made very welcome and the dance was very properly conducted, with a book with names of partners who one would dance with. We made friends with a number of girls and would see them on days off at weekends. Occasionally a group of us would hire a car and go for a picnic or swim in lakes. There was nothing romantic but we enjoyed one another's company, and I maintained correspondence with one of them for forty years afterwards.

Following Tuscaloosa I went on to Gunter Field, Montgomery, for the Basic stage of training. On my second day at Gunter Field there was a funeral, with fourteen coffins for a group of trainees who had flown into a thunderstorm and did not yet have the skills to fly through it. I was a pallbearer and it was a very sombre experience, which brought home the risks of flying, even away from the front line. I understand that of the 10,000 RAF cadets who learnt to fly in the United States during the war, 500 were killed in flying accidents. On a couple of occasions in the USA, flying at night, I ended up in thunderstorms and found them a very anxious experience, but I was able to cope. Later, when I was at Maxwell Field, the Chief Flying Instructor there, Colonel Cy Wilson, had a pre-war B-23 bomber which he would take up when there was a thunderstorm nearby in order to experience it and write advice on what pilots should do to survive.

At Gunter Field we learnt to fly the Vultee BT-13. This had an enclosed cockpit and a more powerful engine than the Stearman trainer. Flying in an enclosed cockpit was like transitioning from a motorbike to a Rolls-Royce. The BT-13 was not unlike a Harvard trainer in character, but with a fixed undercarriage. At Gunter Field we started going on cross-country flights, initially by day and later by night. I had a cockney friend, 'Tramp', who went on one such night flight from Gunter Field and came back late with a crazy story about getting lost and coming across an illuminated figure of a man holding a hammer above his head in the clouds. This seemed wildly implausible but eventually we worked out that he was telling the truth – he'd flown over the city of Birmingham, Alabama, a steel town which has a giant 56-foot cast-iron statue of the god Vulcan placed on a 123-foot pedestal at the top of a nearby mountain that is 3,000 feet high.

It was at Gunter Field that I first became aware that there were RAF pilots among the flying instructors. They were few in number but played a significant part in the training of both American Air Corps pilots and RAF pilots. As luck would have it, I came to be allocated to a RAF pilot, Pilot Officer (PLO) Tween, a nice man and clearly competent in his job. Other British instructors that I recall meeting later were Robin Sinclair (later Lord Thurso), son of the then Secretary of State for Air, and 'Tommy' Thomson, remembered as a senior manager at Schweppes.

From Gunter Field I went back to Turner Field for the final stage of advanced training on twin-engined Curtis AT9s and Cessna AT17s. I was awarded my wings at the completion of this course and we all walked taller such was our pride in the coveted US silver wings. I recall that the general who awarded the wings made a humorous speech about a mother who was watching a similar ceremony and said to her trainee pilot, 'Son, please promise me that you'll fly low and slow' – the worst possible advice to give a young pilot. With the relief of surviving the course, and having proved ourselves fairly competent fliers, we thought this was hilarious. We were then sent to Toronto in Canada to be commissioned as officers in the RAF and to be fitted out in our RAF uniforms. Another proud moment in our lives.

At the completion of the advanced training course I was apparently one of the top five per cent of graduate pilots and was therefore sent back to the US Central Flying School at Maxwell Field, Montgomery, Alabama, where our group trained as instructors with the US Army Air Corps. This was an extremely exacting course, where every fault and weakness in flying discipline had to be straightened out before we qualified under the eagle eyes of the Chief Flying Instructor, Colonel Cy Wilson.

Then with three other instructors I was posted to Moody Field, Valdosta, Georgia. Moody Field was at the south of Georgia, near the border with Florida. The land was low lying and plagued with mosquitoes. The airfield was bordered by swamps and alligators were known to emerge from the swamp and take up residence lying on the runway.

As an instructor I was regularly flying eighty hours a month on T-6s (known in the RAF as Harvards), and the twin-engined AT9, AT10 and AT17. We used Harvards for gunnery practice against ground targets. The aircraft's machine gun was synchronised to fire through the propellers like many of the First World War fighters. It was great fun but one had to be careful; if one dived too steeply and throttled back there was a risk of getting out of synchronisation and firing bullets into the propellers. It was quite usual to fly an aircraft that already had a bullet hole or two in the propeller; they whistled like a banshee – a little disconcerting.

At Moody Field I saw what the American ability to organise on a huge scale could really do. The entire airfield had been constructed in just a few months in 1941, shortly before I arrived. It had a staff of 4,000 running the establishment, and with a fleet of some 170 aircraft it turned out a group of 200 trained pilots every 10 weeks. When the aircraft were due for maintenance they were put on a production line in huge hangars, the cowlings were taken off engines, the aircraft were shampooed and cleaned, and after going through their overhaul the aircraft came out at the far end looking like new. By contrast, when I returned to the United Kingdom and started flying Blenheims at the Advanced Flying Unit at Grantham, I watched maintenance being done on aircraft in the open by a few WAAFs holding buckets of paraffin, cleaning dirty oil off the engines with paint brushes. It all seemed very primitive and amateurish in comparison with what I'd seen in the United States.

Flying in the USA seemed more advanced than Britain in so many respects. Even before the war, planes in the United States navigated by flying on airways with radio beams that connected major airfields and cities. Airways were aerial roadways running between big city airports with radio beams to help you stay on track. The radio beams were supplemented by 'lightways', searchlights placed at ten-mile intervals. In 1940 people were puzzled that the Luftwaffe could find targets like Coventry at night even though the RAF could not find their own targets in Germany. Eventually it was realised that the Germans were setting up similar radio beams for their planes to fly along to their targets, as American military and civil aircraft had been doing for years. Airways as such were virtually unknown back in Britain at the time. When we went on cross-country flights by night or day in the United States, at least one leg would incorporate an airway with a radio range. After a while 'riding the range', as it was de-scribed, became second nature.

While both British and American students were passing through their training together, it fell to my lot to teach Americans only. They were a grand bunch to train: keen and enthusiastic to teach, full of fun and from an extraordinary range of backgrounds and ages. The younger ones aged twenty or so had not long since left high school, while a fair number of older ones had university degrees, and there was I, not yet twenty myself.

One who stood out among the rest was a big man named Grimme, aged about twenty-five. After leaving high school in the hard times at the tail end of the Depression he found employment as a taxi driver in Brooklyn, New York. His knowledge of the wicked world was a source of entertainment for all around him and would have filled chapters of anecdotes for Damon Runyon's books, which were so popular at the time. I hope that he survived the war, but many of our graduates went on to fly B17s and B24s in the Eighth Air Force during the difficult days of 1943 and early 1944 when so many were lost.

I made two or three very good friends in the Air Force as time went by. One of them, John Ethrington, was another instructor at Moody Field, who survived the war and became a doctor in Canada.

Another very close friend, John Metcalfe, also trained and worked with me as an instructor at Moody Field. When we returned to England I was the best man at his wedding to a girl he'd known in England before he went to the US for training. John later flew Mosquito night intruder fighters that were used to attack traffic on German roads and airfields, and a few weeks after his wedding he was killed when his aircraft hit a hill in Belgium. While I was working at Moody Field, John and I went to Daytona Beach where we were friendly with a WAAC officer, Natalie Yates, whose husband David had been captured by the Japanese when they invaded the

Philippines. She didn't find out what happened to him for several years until the Philippines was liberated and she received a message that he was arriving by boat in the US. While a prisoner he sought out another captive who spoke Russian and set about learning Russian, as he thought that knowledge of the language would come in handy after the war. It did, and he became a colonel in Army Intelligence. Natalie and I stayed in touch for many years after the war and I met David when he was stationed at an American Army base at Wiesbaden in Germany. Years later David took me on a visit to the military academy at West Point where in retirement he lectured in Russian.

While I was at Moody Field, a friend of mine, Ken Stewart, was due to return to the United Kingdom via Canada, and was sent a cheque to cover his rail fare from Georgia to Toronto. Ken had bought a car and instead of purchasing the train ticket used the cheque to pay off his debts on the car. Instructors were permitted to use planes on days off to build up flying hours, provided we didn't go more than 1,000 miles, so Ken asked me if I could borrow a plane and drop him off in Toronto. I agreed to help out, but the day before we were due to go my commanding officer told me that I couldn't go because I was needed to keep up the flying schedule at the base. I managed to find other instructors to cover for me so flew up to Toronto with Ken. When we landed at the main airport we were told that a taxi into the city would cost a $30 fare. This seemed a lot of money at the time. There was a small airport on an island in the centre of the city, so we flew there to save the taxi fare. Before I returned to Moody Field the next day I was presented with a bill for $7.25 for parking my aircraft, which I still have today. When I got back to Moody Field I was confronted by my CO, who was not happy about my jaunt up to Canada in defiance of his orders – I was lucky to get off with just a mild reprimand. It did raise the issue of how far one should go to help a friend.

Two months before I returned to England my friend Ken met a girl in the nearby town of Valdosta and invited me to meet her sister, Corrine Briggs-Smith. We fell deeply in love. She seemed to reflect all that was good in an American small-town girl: to my eyes beautiful, with a lovely personality, and from a laughter-filled family. However, it was totally impractical to arrange for her to come to England while war was on. I was also troubled by what the future would hold for me and my family because of the war, and particularly who would look after my brother John in later life.

Thus it was that I then left the vibrant, young and exciting United States, and my lovely Corrine, in a very sad frame of mind, and came back to an uncertain future in England. Corrine and I continued to correspond, and each of her letters to me were illustrated with marvellous watercolour headings. Back in England, in the ordinary course of social life from time to time I met other girls, but Corrine's face was always in the background. When I returned from my adventures I wrote to her to tell her what had happened to me and to rediscover something of her life. My letter came back with a note on the envelope, 'No longer at this address', written in what I recognised as Corrine's hand. This was very painful for me at the time, as I'm sure it was for her, but it was a sign that the world had moved on.

Chapter 6

Returning to England

In November 1943 I was due to return to the United Kingdom. I sailed from Halifax, Canada, to the Clyde on the *Queen Elizabeth,* along with 17,000 other passengers, including an entire US infantry division and 1,000 airmen. There were six men in each single cabin and when we boarded we were given a ticket with mealtimes twelve hours apart that we were scheduled to attend – I considered myself lucky to have been allocated 9 a.m. and 9 p.m! We didn't starve between meals as there was a PX shop on board supplying small items. I remember the PA on the ship broadcasting statements like 'No gambling on this ship' – which were conspicuously ignored. You couldn't take two steps on the boat without stumbling on some form of gambling. This time the crossing of the Atlantic only took five days in comparison to the fourteen-day ordeal when I came across on the *Montcalm.*

I had been in the United States almost two

years. Coming home as a qualified pilot, my time as an instructor meant that I had logged more flying hours than experienced pilots flying on operational squadrons. I was more self-assured and comfortable with giving orders than I had been as a cadet, although I don't think that I was ever the school prefect type. I preferred the relative informality of the RAF to the strictness I experienced in the training environment in the USAAF, which modelled itself on West Point, and insisted on creased trousers, shined shoes and a highly prescriptive standard of conduct; this environment may not have been characteristic of the USAAF operational squadrons. Generally speaking, the degree of formality and enforcement of rules and regulations declined the closer one got to the front line.

On arrival I went home to see my family in Southwick. Life was noticeably harder during wartime for ordinary people. Food rationing was a constant worry and one could only buy clothes if one had the coupons. There was little petrol for cars. The blackout and continuing bomb damage – especially with the V1 campaign that commenced just after D-Day in June 1944 – combined to make life difficult. They seemed to be coping reasonably well with the consequences of the war, notwithstanding the stress of keeping the family furniture business going. They were also worried about my brother, Roger, who was away at sea with the Merchant Navy and constantly at risk of having his ship mined or torpedoed. My sister Betty's husband, Wing Commander Jimmy Pike, had been a pre-war career officer in the

RAF. He now commanded a squadron of Flying Fortresses based in the Azores that was part of Coastal Command's forces patrolling the Atlantic against U-boats.

On my return to England one immediately noticed the number of American servicemen who were now based there in the lead up to D-Day. I liked Americans myself, and wasn't too worried that they were bowling over English women, but the disparity in pay between them and the lowly paid British armed forces did lead to friction.

It was significant to see how many jobs that were formerly done by men were now being undertaken by women. Women worked in aircraft and munitions factories; they drove buses and underground trains in London; they drove hospital ambulances; and they served as air-raid wardens. You name it, they did it, to a degree not dreamt of before the war. My impression was that the proportion of women in the workforce was far higher in wartime Britain than in the United States. 'While much of this work simply had to be done, hard though it might have been, one could see that it was an important factor in the social changes likely to occur after the war. Against the background of the long years of the Depression women were at last able to earn money for themselves and develop a sense of independence as never before.

After a period of leave I was sent to a holding depot at Harrogate in Yorkshire. Because I had almost 1,000 hours of flying experience I was given the choice whether to operate fighters or bombers. I understand that the RAF used psychological testing to determine a pilot's aptitude for either bombers or fighters, with the more aggressive and individualistic being directed towards the former category. I was identified as a prospective bomber pilot, but because of my experience in the early years of the war, seeing the German raids on England, I liked the idea of a defensive role and expressed a preference for a posting to night fighters.

I went to a Night-fighter Advanced Flying Unit at RAF Spitalgate, near Grantham, where I started a six-week course flying Blenheims. I had done quite a bit of night flying in the United States but becoming acclimatised to flying in blacked-out England was a challenge. In the blackout one could just make out some geographical features such as rivers, lakes and coastlines. Although there was also the ability to use flashing beacons to help navigate, and Air Traffic Control (ATC) could give some help with bearings to steer, the transition was far from easy. Nonetheless it was gratifying to find my logbook stamped 'Above Average' at the completion of the course.

At this time the RAF advertised for those seeking permanent commissions and I applied. I was interviewed by a very fierce Air Vice-Marshal Champion de Crespigny who was Air Officer Commanding No. 21 Training Group. He asked me general questions like 'What books do you read?' I mentioned T.E. Lawrence's *Seven Pillars of Wisdom* and this sparked lengthy reminiscences of his encounters with Lawrence of Arabia during the First World War. I recall that he did almost all the talking so I'm not sure how he formed a view of my talents.

When I completed the Advanced Flying Unit course there was no night-fighter squadron that I could be sent to as the existing ones were not suffering high losses and no new ones were being formed. After going on leave I was therefore sent back to Grantham, and did the Advanced Flying Unit course over again to keep in practice. My friend David Russell was in the British Army's First Airborne Division, based at a nearby airfield called Barkstone Heath, so I was able to meet him in Grantham. Together with a couple of WAAFs we celebrated my twenty-first birthday on 4 July 1944 with a good dinner at The George in Grantham and cigars in the Mess afterwards. The First Airborne were on standby in case they were needed for the invasion of France (they weren't) and remained on almost permanent standby as the British Army advanced across France after D-Day. When they finally did go into action in Operation Market Garden (the story of which was told in the book and movie *A Bridge Too Far*) in September 1944 it was the thirteenth time they'd been on standby.

At RAF Spitalgate we maintained a war map in the intelligence office and we were rostered on to make updates to it. On 6 June 1944 it fell to me to put American and British flags on the map to mark the landings on Normandy beaches. These were exciting times, but I felt my own contribution to the war effort was less than I wanted.

Shortly after D-Day my friend John Ethrington and I, with a couple of others, went down to 8

Group Headquarters at Huntingdon for an interview, hoping to join the Pathfinders. The 8 Group Pathfinders were elite squadrons within Bomber Command that were responsible for marking targets for the main heavy bomber groups to aim at. I was interviewed by the selection officer, Group Captain Hamish Mahaddie. He asked me, 'Why do you want to join the Pathfinders?'

I told him that I wanted to get into action, that I wanted to fly Mosquitoes, and I was interested in the technical side of the Pathfinders' role, particularly the Oboe navigational system for which my beam flying experience in the United States might prove useful.

Mahaddie told me that as I had done over 1,000 hours' flying they would take me on in the Light Night Striking Force (LNSF), which formed part of 8 Group Pathfinders, but I would have to do a tour of forty-five operations with the LNSF before I could join one of the Pathfinder squadrons responsible for precision marking of targets. The LNSF were Pathfinder squadrons flying Mosquito bombers which, as well as precision bombing specific targets in Germany, were often sent off in groups to draw off night fighters from the main bomber force of Lancaster, Halifax and Stirling heavy bombers. Our Mosquito bombers carried a single 4,000-pound bomb (known as a 'cookie'), said to be capable of taking off the roofs of houses within a radius of about 400 yards, so a force of say fifty aircraft could do a lot of damage. I wouldn't get my Pathfinder badge until I'd completed this first tour with the LNSF.

When I initially chose to train to fly night fighters this decision was partly influenced by the knowledge that losses for night fighters were less than those for bombers. In changing to the Pathfinders I knew that I was moving to a riskier area, although it was common knowledge that losses in the LNSF were slightly lower than the high losses experienced elsewhere in the RAF. Flying an unarmed aircraft made of plywood over enemy territory sounds suicidal, but the Mosquito relied on speed to evade enemy defences. I also understood that the LNSF experienced around two per cent losses for each operation, rather than the five per cent loss rate that was common for Bomber Command as a whole for most of the war. A five per cent loss rate meant that the odds of successfully completing a tour of thirty operations were less than even.

Like others I wanted to play a more active role in the war and perhaps advance my career prospects in the RAF. My friends and I all knew the risks but we wished to get into the action and do our part. I had heard all about the Mosquito aircraft from other pilots and was greatly taken with stories about its speed and the precision raids that Mosquito squadrons had undertaken. In February 1944, eighteen Mosquitoes, led by Group Captain Frank Pickard, had carried out an audacious low-level attack on Amiens prison. Pickard and his aircraft were lost but the raid was reported in all the newspapers as a triumph; the precision bombing successfully breached the prison walls and enabled imprisoned Resistance members to escape. Although not an 8 Group operation it gained much publicity at the time. I wanted to fly Mosquitoes, in any role.

Chapter 7

The Air War

I had followed the reporting of the air war in the papers, radio and newsreels with great interest. I was a diligent newspaper reader and the air war was prominent in them with regular reports on targets that had been bombed and articles on noteworthy exploits by particular crews. I bought a radio while in the United States and this was another source of information, particularly from the coverage of the US Eighth Air Force's arrival in England. We all knew that the media put a positive slant on their coverage, for instance portraying Dunkirk as something of a triumph when one knew it signalled a significant defeat. Generally the public were aware of the extent of the grim losses that were being suffered on a daily basis. What we were not conscious of was that this immense sacrifice was not even resulting in accurate or effective bombing in the first few years of the war.

During the 'phoney war' the resources of Bomber Command had been devoted to dropping leaflets over Germany and a few abortive raids on the German Navy. The Government's instruction to avoid any raid that might harm German civilians limited the potential targets. This all changed when the war became a life or death struggle for Britain following the fall of France. It was soon apparent that the aircraft flown by Bomber Command – the Fairey Battle and Bristol Blenheim medium bombers and the Handley Page Hampden, Armstrong Whitley and Vickers Wellington heavy bombers – were too vulnerable to enemy fighters and anti-aircraft fire to be able to conduct the daytime raids that the pre-war Bomber Command had planned and trained for.

As a result, from late 1940 the obsolete medium bombers were largely retired from daylight operations (apart from anti-shipping strikes in the Channel and North Sea). The heavy bombers that were then in operation – which actually only carried a load of 3,000–4,000lb, less than the load that I would later carry in my Mosquito – were restricted to night bombing. For the rest of the war Bomber Command largely focused on night-time raids on Occupied Europe and Germany. At first aircraft losses were substantially less than during the daytime raids because the German night-time defences were largely unprepared at this stage in the war. The downside of night raids for the RAF was the lack of aids to navigation and consequent inability to plot a course accurately. Bombers were expected to navigate by following compass directions given to the pilot on take-off, and using landmarks on the ground below, supplemented by taking sightings from the stars using a sextant if the night was clear and the pilot was able to fly straight and level for long enough. These methods were completely unreliable. In his history *Bomber Command,* Max Hastings tells the story of one occasion where a crew became disorientated and dropped their bombs on what they thought was a German airfield, but shortly afterwards they realised to their dismay that they had mistaken the Thames Estuary for the estuary of the Rhine and dropped their bombs on a British Fighter Command station in Cambridgeshire. Two Spitfires from the Fighter Command station they had bombed returned the favour by dropping Iron Crosses over the home airfield of the wayward bomber and the unfortunate pilot was demoted and acquired the nickname 'Baron Von Warren'.

After the war I heard directly a similar story from my friend Bob Hodges (later Air Marshal Sir Lewis Hodges) who was flying a Hampden bomber in 1940. After bombing what he believed to be the city of Stettin deep in Germany, while returning he was forced to crash-land through lack of fuel. Bob thought that when he came down he had at least made it back to England. However, when the crew got out they found they were 100 miles off course and had come down in Brittany in Occupied France. Bob was able to evade capture and make his way back to England via Marseilles and the escape line for airmen in which Nancy Wake was much involved.

The RAF's propaganda in films like *Target for Tonight,* which I saw in 1941 before I went to the United States (and featured Group Captain Pickard from the Amiens raid as the pilot of a

Wellington bomber), suggested we were inflicting serious damage on the Germans. In fact, Bomber Command knew that the difficulties for planes in finding targets and then accurately marking them meant that the RAF was not bombing with sufficient precision to achieve any strategic objectives in 1940 and 1941. Around a third of aircraft returned to base without having actually located and attacked their primary target. The problems with precision bombing were confirmed by a report in August 1941 by Mr D.M. Butt of the Cabinet Secretariat on the performance of Bomber Command against targets in France and Germany. This report analysed the targets and reports from the two-thirds of aircraft that claimed to have attacked their primary target and found that only one-third of aircraft came within five miles of their targets. This proportion fell to one-tenth in respect of attacks on the Ruhr, the industrial area in the west of Germany, which was a major target for the RAF throughout the war. The Government knew that the position was likely to worsen as German defences strengthened, and made raids on moonlit nights, when greater levels of bombing accuracy might be achieved, more difficult.

In the absence of a second front in Europe, Bomber Command attacks were seen as the principal way for Britain to take the war to Germany. Immediately after the fall of France the intention was still to avoid civilian casualties. The Government's revised instructions to the Air Ministry in June 1940 required that bombing 'must be made with reasonable care to avoid undue loss of civil life in the vicinity of the target'. However, the blitzing of London, Coventry, Portsmouth and other cities made Churchill less concerned about the prospect of civilian German casualties and more receptive to a policy of area bombing. In December 1940 Churchill stated: 'I consider the rapid expansion of the bomber force one of the greatest military objectives now before us.' A substantial part of the British economy was devoted to manufacturing the new heavy bombers – the Short Stirling, Handley Page Halifax and Avro Lancaster – that would enable this expansion. Bomber Command planned to have 4,000 heavy bombers and looked to new technology to solve the navigation problems. There was a temporary slowdown in the bomber offensive over late 1941/early 1942. Then in spring 1942 Bomber Command, under a new commander, Sir Arthur Harris, introduced new aircraft, an updated policy of area bombing, and the latest bombing techniques. These techniques involved the lead bombers marking the objectives with flares, which the main bombing force would then target with incendiaries and high explosives.

These techniques also utilised 'Gee', a navigation system involving radio transmitter stations in England sending pulses which, when received by the bomber aircraft, allowed the aircraft to plot its position. Gee provided accurate locations to within about 165 yards at short ranges and up to a mile at longer ranges over Germany. Unlike the beam systems used by the Germans to guide their bombers to cities like Coventry – which I had used myself when flying in the United States – Gee pulses were radiated in all directions, so even if detected, they would not reveal the bombers' likely destinations. A limitation of Gee was its vulnerability to being jammed by the Germans. There was a six-month period after its introduction in March 1942 before the Germans discovered how to do this. During this time Harris planned and executed the first RAF 1,000-bomber raid over Cologne.

The introduction of Gee was part of a technology race between the British and Germans, with first one side, and then the other, introducing new measures that conferred a temporary advantage in the battle. In December 1942 the British introduced 'Oboe', an even more accurate blind-bombing device. A bomber flew along a circle of electronic pulses defined by one transmitting station in England – known as the 'Cat' – and dropped its load (either bombs, or marking flares, depending on the mission) when it reached the intersection with the circle defined by another station, known as 'Mouse'. Oboe was extraordinarily accurate, with an error radius of about 120 yards at a range of 250 miles. Like Gee it was vulnerable to jamming by the Germans and its main limitation was that its range only extended to the Ruhr, although this was extended later in the war when stations were established in France after D-Day. Shortly afterwards Bomber Command introduced the H2S airborne radar, which gave the navigator operating the set some idea of the ground below. H2S could be used on targets like Berlin that were outside the range of

Gee and Oboe, but the results it gave were often unclear and the Germans developed a Naxos radar detector that enabled German night fighters to home in on the bomber using an H2S set. At about the same time that I started flying operationally in August 1944, the RAF introduced a new system called LORAN (Long Range Navigation), a radio navigation system similar in principle to Gee but with a greater range.

Even with Gee and H2S, navigation was still challenging. When I was flying, Gee coverage ran out east of the Ruhr and we relied on Pathfinders with H2S to guide us into targets in Berlin. Returning from one raid our Gee readings seemed doubtful and we heard other planes experiencing the same problem and calling radio stations back in England to get new bearings. My navigator Ron called a station, code named 'Largetype',[3] which turned out to be Manston in Kent. He was given a bearing that showed that, instead of being over the Dutch coast as we thought, we were further south over the French coast near Calais. When we returned to our base we found that a jet stream – air currents that flow west to east above 23,000 feet – had taken us about 70 miles south of our intended course. We had not even known about jet streams before this incident and our windspeed for the last one and a half hours had been of the order of north-west at 140 knots.

A further much simpler piece of technology used by Bomber Command was Window, being small thin strips of aluminium foil that were dropped by aircraft to swamp the German radar system with false readings so that they could not pick out individual aircraft or the size of the attacking force. Window was first used in Operation Gomorrah, the Hamburg series of raids that began on 24 July 1943, which created a firestorm that destroyed more than eight square miles of the city and killed an estimated 40,000 people. We carried Window in our aircraft on some occasions and dropped it in particular locations to lead the German defences to believe that we were part of a much larger force.

Each of these innovations gave Bomber Command some temporary advantage in the battle against the formidable German defences, and the tonnage of bombs dropped over Germany continued to increase between 1942 and early 1944. After the Hamburg strikes and a campaign of raids on targets in the Ruhr in 1943, Harris believed that he had the advantage, and the German Armaments Minister, Albert Speer, acknowledged that 'Hamburg had put the fear of God into me.' Speer also expressed the opinion that if the Hamburg raid was repeated elsewhere within three months, Germany would have to sue for peace. Harris launched an offensive at Berlin over the winter of 1943/44 with the objective of doing just this. However, the bombers were not able to deliver the knockout blow that the RAF was hoping for and over 1,000 RAF aircraft were lost during this period. The Germans had their own technological innovations such as radar-controlled anti-aircraft guns and searchlights, and night fighters with cannon firing upwards so they could fire into heavy bombers from directly below, where the bombers had no defensive armament.

71

Even while I was in the United States it was common knowledge that Lancasters and Halifaxes had a very high loss rate. When I returned to the United Kingdom I gained a clearer picture of the front-line Bomber Command experience through talking to other airmen and reading the confidential reports available in the intelligence rooms located in all RAF stations. I was told that Sir Arthur Harris was nicknamed 'Butch' or 'Butcher Harris' because of Bomber Command's enormous losses. I learnt from the other men on my squadron that trips to Berlin (the Big City) were regarded with trepidation. One heard about the raid on Nuremberg early in 1944, when Bomber Command had lost ninety-five aircraft in one night. After that raid, and the lack of success against Berlin, Bomber Command reluctantly had to switch to bombing in preparation for D-Day and subsequently to raids in support of the Army as it sought to liberate France. In assisting the Army, a lot of bombing was carried out in daylight when the bombers were more vulnerable to German day fighters. At the same time Bomber Command was also targeting V1 sites in the Pas-de-Calais. From my friend 'Benny' Goodman, a pilot in one of the Mosquitoes marking for the raid, I heard about a big attack on a military camp at Mailly-le-Camp in May 1944 where 42 of the 362 bomber aircraft were lost when German fighters got into the bomber stream.[4]

When I joined an operational squadron in August 1944, morale was higher than it had been at the peak of the Berlin offensive in early 1944 as the balance seemed to be tilting in our favour.

In spring 1944 the USAF had targeted raids on the German aircraft industry, hoping to weaken the German day-fighter force opposing the American bomber formations and their Mustang fighter escorts. This effectively resulted in the destruction of the German day fighters, at least in terms of trained and experienced personnel. While night defences were still strong, when attacks on targets in Germany resumed in August 1944 we thought that we were now winning the war in the air as well as on the ground. In September 1944, losses fell to 96 aircraft missing for 6,428[5] sorties. I was also fortunate to be flying Mosquitoes, unarmed but faster than most German night fighters, and also less vulnerable to anti-aircraft fire than the heavy bombers flying in streams – or so one thought!

Chapter 8

Flying Mosquitoes

Because Mosquitoes operated at altitudes of up to 30,000 feet, it was thought necessary to put aircrew through tests in a decompression chamber to ensure that we were not susceptible to the bends. We were lectured on the consequences of the bends, which can painfully occur due to bubbles of gases forming in the body as a result of change in pressure, either through ascending from depth (in the case of deep-sea diving) or ascending to altitude. We were warned on the precautions that one needed to take to avoid such attacks. I recall being told that before flying one should avoid eating what was described as 'farinaceous' food, i.e. such things as potatoes and beans, which were high in starch. It is noteworthy that the one group who were not given this advice were the cooks at the airfield one flew from. Thus for our usual night-flying suppers before raids we were given our favourite plates of bacon and eggs on fried bread, with lashings of chips and baked beans. My navigator and I had no cause to complain at this diet (which was more lavish than was available to most people in heavily rationed Great Britain) and we certainly did not suffer aching joints or other symptoms of the bends.

After passing the decompression chamber test I was posted to the headquarters of 8 Group at Wyton airfield near Huntingdon. Wyton was a pre-war airfield and our accommodation was in a pre-war married-quarters house next to the residence of the Air Officer Commanding 8 Group, the Australian Don Bennett. Bennett insisted on interviewing every new pilot in 8 Group and had a ten to fifteen-minute discussion with me when I joined. A few weeks later, when I was walking around the perimeter track at the airfield, his car pulled over and he asked me, 'Hello Dell, how are you getting on?' Not many commanding officers could do that after a ten-minute chat.

Like others, I had a very high regard for Bennett, and in my judgement he was one of the best of all the Bomber Command hierarchy. He was an Australian former airline pilot, and it was said

74

that he had written a textbook on navigation during his honeymoon! He didn't suffer fools and insisted that all his aircrew shared his aggressive attitude.

I had a further encounter with Bennett at a later date when I was with my squadron. We were told at a midday briefing that an operation was planned that night, but the weather forecast was bad and it was unlikely that the planned operation would proceed. That evening during our briefing we heard a Mosquito land at our airfield in cloud and rain and shortly afterwards Bennett came into the briefing room wearing his flying gear. Bennett said that he'd flown from the Ruhr in the east, to Dublin in the west. There was a cold front over us moving east and the weather would be OK at base by the time of our return. This news was greeted with loud groans from the assembled aircrew, but that was the sort of chap he was. We respected that.

All aircrew were volunteers and a very hard line was taken with anyone suspected of shirking operations – or 'Lacking Moral Fibre' (LMF) as it was officially termed. I didn't directly come across any such cases myself, but heard that anyone suspected of LMF would immediately be taken out of circulation. I was told of one pilot who had cut short a mission because he thought one of his engines was giving trouble, though still running. He was sent for and sacked on the spot; this seems a little extreme so there may have been some previous history.

That is not to say that we were gung-ho, or stridently aggressive; we didn't hide our dislike of high-risk targets like Berlin. I know that heavy bomber crews were preoccupied with calculating the odds of surviving a tour of operations – which in their case were less than even throughout much of the war. Mosquito pilots faced better odds so we weren't quite as worried.

I did my first training on Mosquitoes from the nearby airfield of Warboys, near Huntingdon, which was a Mosquito Conversion Unit 1655. There were ten pilots and ten navigators on our course. I chose to pair up with a navigator called Ron Naiff, who immediately struck me as being a good sort of chap. Ron was a very nice fellow, a man about my height with a ruddy complexion; he had a good sense of humour but was also serious minded. He had won a place at St Andrews in Scotland to read law so we had a Scottish university connection in common. We were about the same age but Ron had already done one tour of operations (thirty ops directed at enemy targets), flying as a navigator on Short Stirlings. The Stirling was a heavy bomber that had a bad reputation among aircrew. They flew at a lower altitude than Halifaxes and Lancasters because their engines were underpowered if they tried to fly above 10,000–12,000 feet, and this meant they were more vulnerable to flak and enemy fighters. Lancaster crews would cheer if they were told there were Stirlings flying with them on a raid as the German defences would concentrate on attacking the low-flying Stirlings, thereby improving the Lancasters' own chances of survival. Ron told me that on one occasion his crew came back with incendiary bombs stuck on the wings of their

Stirling, which had been dropped by the Lancasters and Halifaxes bombing above them. I also heard that when approaching the target Stirling crews would put one crew member into the Perspex astrodome on top of the fuselage so they could look up to check that there were no Lancasters or Halifaxes above them. If there were, they would know they needed to take evasive action.

I remember Ron saying that, 'What we've been through has been utter madness', and he planned to work for a year or two on a farm after the war in order to regain his grip on reality. He was a very brave man; once I got to know him well I noticed that a very slight twitch to one of his eyes showed something of the strain he had been under. He soldiered on nevertheless. It was not unusual among aircrew to develop what was known as 'the twitch'.

The Mosquito was regarded in the RAF as a prestigious, cutting-edge aircraft, faster than anything else flying at that time, and the better odds of survival relative to the heavy bombers made it an attractive proposition to fly. I recently had the great privilege of seeing the only Mosquito in the world currently flying at the Ardmore Air Show in Auckland, New Zealand, on 29 September 2012. Along with a number of other former Mosquito pilots I was invited to witness a newly rebuilt Mark 26 take part in the show. I was given the opportunity to climb up the telescopic ladder leading to the crew hatch and step into the cockpit, and it was then that the memories came flooding back. It was quite a moment. Everything was as I remembered it: the instrument panel, the crew seats slightly staggered so the pilot's shoulder did not touch the navigator's. Even the smell was right, a particular mixture of paint, glue and cellulose. The Mosquito's Merlin engines have a characteristic crackle as the aircraft taxies on the runway, and hearing this sound at Ardmore brought back many wartime recollections. After taking off the Mosquito made a number of low-level passes just above the crowd, wheeling gracefully at each end. Again it was the sound, the distinctive roar of the twin Merlins in flight, which stirred the soul. Marvellous!

On my first flight in 1944 I was struck right away by the elegance of the Mosquito; it handled beautifully compared to the Blenheims that I had been flying in my night-fighter training. One could forget the risks of our role and feel grateful to the British taxpayer for putting such a high-performance aircraft in the hands of a 21-year-old. It was a pleasure to fly, with well-arranged instruments and everything conveniently to hand. The Mosquito had some characteristics to guard against: with two Merlin engines of 1,635 horsepower each, it tended to swing to the left on takeoff. I also found that when coming into land one had to get used to the higher approach speed. Another negative of the Mosquito was the struggle in getting out of the cockpit if the aircraft got into difficulties. The hatchway that gave access was below the floor on the starboard side, not far from the starboard engine and its propeller. One could open a hatch in the Perspex roof, but if one tried to get out this way during flight one was likely to be blown back against the tailplane, with dire consequences.

My instructor was Flight Lieutenant 'Benny' Goodman, an experienced airman who'd flown heavy bombers before doing another tour with a Pathfinder squadron flying Mosquitoes. We had two to three hours' flying in a Mosquito with dual controls on 31 July and 3 August, before my first solo flight on 3 August 1944. As part of our training we did long-distance training runs to Land's End, up to Scotland and Ireland, flying out to sea to the islet of Rockall, and doing dummy bombing runs on a target range in Lincolnshire. Most of it was night flying. Additionally the navigators spent their time in the classroom practising with the Gee navigation system and setting up bombsights, as they were also responsible for the bomb aiming.

In our free time, together with my friend John Etherington, I arranged to meet a couple of sisters, Betty and Pam, together with their parents, at the Bridge pub in Huntingdon. When we arrived we found the girls had befriended another girl waiting to have dinner with a pilot on our training course. He did not turn up for the meal and they asked me to help contact him. When I rang the Duty Officer at Warboys I was told that his plane had not come back from a training flight. It fell to me to break the news to the girl that her boyfriend was overdue and missing. All three girls were in floods of tears and when we came to leave it became clear that a special relationship had formed between Betty and John, and Pam and myself, as a consequence. These things tended to happen in wartime because we were all conscious of the uncertain future we faced.

When Ron and I had completed the long-distance bombing runs we were posted to 692 Squadron based at Graveley, near Huntingdon, Cambridgeshire. This was a wartime station and its facilities were very different from what we had enjoyed at a pre-war station like Wyton. Wyton had an Officers' Mess that resembled a gentlemen's club; the Mess at Graveley was an enlarged Nissen hut, comfortably furnished but pretty basic, and our accommodation was also in Nissen huts. I was allocated a bed that had been occupied by 'Dickie' Bird, a pilot I had met during our training course. Sent to the squadron a couple of days before me he had already gone missing on his very first operation. This brought home the risks of operational service, even though at this stage of the war, as the Allied armies were breaking out of the Normandy beachhead, many thought that the war would be over by Christmas.

The commanding officer of 692 Squadron was Wing Commander Joe Northrop, who stood out as an old man at twenty-eight and was regarded with a certain amount of awe by us youngsters on the squadron. Joe was one of those who had gone to the Halton Technical School for RAF apprentices in pre-war years for training as mechanics and engineers. When I was a schoolboy my parents had considered sending me to Halton, but instead I got a scholarship to Dover. Later in life I came to regret missing this opportunity to learn all about the technical details of aircraft.

Once war was declared, like many Halton graduates, Joe obtained training as a pilot. He was a man of considerable character and competence. He'd often come on operations with us and was well regarded.

The squadron had eighteen aircraft at total strength, divided into two flights each with a flight commander who was a squadron leader or flight lieutenant. Normally a certain number of crews from the squadron, say twelve, would fly out on an operation. While we would be rostered to try to avoid crews doing bombing trips on two or three successive nights, sometimes this became necessary.

The rest of the squadron were a mix of men from Australia (the Australians stood out because they wore Royal Australian Air Force (RAAF) navy blue rather than the standard RAF blue), Norway, and Canada, as well as Britain. Quite a high proportion of the aircrew had done previous tours. It was the practice to give officers the DFC and non-commissioned aircrew the DFM simply for the achievement of surviving an operational tour, and one noticed a number of these ribbons on the uniforms around the squadron. There was a very different feeling in the Mess from what I'd been used to. This showed itself in hard drinking and a lot of frivolity and jollification as a form of escapism from the pressure that everyone was under, but when there was business to be done, it was carried out with due diligence. At the stage I joined, there were relatively few losses on Mosquitoes, morale was high, and there was the feeling that the war was going well, with much confidence in both Butch Harris and the RAF command. We all got on well and drank a lot of beer.

There was a strong sense of comradeship within our squadron. We were all facing the same threats and sharing similar experiences on a day-to-day basis. This comradeship was something different from close friendship. The nature of service in the RAF meant that aircrew did not spend a long length of time together, as men completed their tours of operations or perhaps failed to come back. Of the men on the squadron, I was really only emotionally close to Ron; I felt very much part of a team of two with him. We each had our clearly defined duties in navigating and flying the Mosquito and I felt an acute responsibility to bring him back safely.

Ron told me that on his tour on Stirlings, not only did the crew develop a strong sense of comradeship among themselves, they also became very attached to their faithful aircraft, which brought them home unscathed. He said it was not unknown for them to go aboard and play cards in its voluminous fuselage on rainy days!

Our operational flights were relatively brief in duration and there was only limited non-operational flying; we'd take the aircraft up for a brief check every few days. One of my prevailing memories of my time on the squadron was the feeling of boredom, trying to find ways to occupy my mind between operations. It was very different from the long, busy days as an instructor in the United States. The RAF recognised that we had time on our hands and ran lectures and talks on topics such as new ways of navigating and escaping techniques if we were shot down. We seemed to spend a lot of our day sitting around, reading, sleeping and playing cards. Sometimes we were able to take part in the odd game of rugby or soccer, and two or three evenings a week we could leave the base to go to the pub or the cinema. Whenever we went out people were very friendly to us and seemed conscious of the risks we ran on an operational squadron. There appeared to be widespread public support for what Bomber Command was doing. I was not aware at the time of anyone raising concerns over the morality of the bombing campaign against Germany.

We didn't like the Germans, of course, and regarded them as a pretty ruthless lot, but there were different degrees of dislike for them within the RAF. At one extreme was someone like Douglas Bader who hated the Germans with a passion. I heard a story after the war about Bader's arrival at Stalag Luft III after he'd been captured by the Germans: when he entered the camp the Germans laid on a guard of honour but Bader responded in a rather insulting way, pretending to inspect the guard of honour and finding fault with their dress and deportment. This incensed the senior British officer there, 'Wings' Day, because he was absolutely correct in the way he dealt with Germans. Most of us just went about our flying business normally but in the backs of our minds one did not forgive the Germans for bombing London and Coventry or for my part, the death of our butcher's delivery boy at Southwick nor the old lady in her kitchen in Kingston lane.

Chapter 9

My First Operation

I joined 692 Squadron on 28 August 1944 and went on my first operation over Hamburg on 29 August. After almost three years of training I was very keyed up for this mission. Not so much looking forward to it, but definitely feeling that I was ready for it.

The normal routine was that at about midday one would find out that an operation was planned for the evening and whether one was on it. All of the missions that I flew were night-time operations; the squadron may have done a few daytime raids while I was there but not any involving me. I had experienced a lot of night flying, and had logged many flight hours as an instructor, so night operations were not a problem.

We would check the aircraft allocated to us and do a quick test flight during the day, before attending a briefing in the evening when we would be told where we were going. Normally the briefing was quite late, an hour or so before we took off, at 11p.m. or later. We would have an anxious wait sitting around in the Officers' Mess, sometimes reading newspapers or writing letters. There was a directive to leave a letter to one's next of kin before departing on an operation. I had written such a letter and it was duly sent to my parents, where I found it when I eventually returned to England. I recall that in it I thanked them for everything that they'd done for me.

The briefing was always quite tense, some targets being regarded as tougher than others. Berlin was considered particularly taxing because it was a long way there, the city's defences were very tough, and it was at the extreme range of our aircraft. If Berlin was the target it was quite usual to have fuel gauges reading zero by the time one reached the Dutch coast on the return trip. Although we were advised that we still had about forty minutes' flying time left when the fuel gauges were reading zero, our confidence in the reliability of gauges was low. There were emergency airfields with long runways close to the east coast of England for planes to use in these circumstances. I landed once at Woodbridge in Suffolk and once at Manston in Kent because I doubted that I had enough fuel to get back to Graveley. The night that I landed at Manston airfield at 2 a.m. I found the airfield chock-a-block with gliders and tow aircraft for Operation Market Garden, when the First Airborne Division were dropped to secure bridges over the Rhine at Arnhem. This operation commenced on 17 September 1944.

One had to get kitted up before operations. Aircrew in heavy bombers wore flying suits for warmth, but the Mosquito was fairly airtight and well heated so I just wore our normal battledress uniform with a thick navy blue issue sweater underneath, known as a 'frock flying' because of its long length. A Mae West inflatable life jacket went on over my battledress. We were told not to take any personal belongings on an operation, so would turn out our pockets to ensure that we did not have letters or anything else that might be useful for the enemy if we were shot down. Security was constantly drummed into us. We were forbidden to talk to anyone off base about targets we might have visited. I recall the barman in the local pub commenting on the activity on our airfield based on what he'd observed of aircraft testing engines. I now know that the Germans listened in to our radio frequencies, and by hearing aircraft testing radios during the day got some indication that there would be a raid that night.

We wore fleece-lined black suede flying boots referred to as the 'escape type' as the shoe part could be cut off from the uppers. An earlier version of these boots had zips but these were dispensed with as they tended to fall off if one had to parachute out, leaving one to land in one's socks – not conducive to a successful escape. The shoe part of the boots had laces so that it looked like a normal shoe.

Next I put on white silk gloves – we also had leather gauntlets but I chose not to wear them as they were clumsy. Finally I put on my leather flying helmet, with an electric lead from a microphone to the aircraft's radio, and an oxygen mask that was coupled up to the aircraft's oxygen system.

Once we were kitted up Ron and I, together with another two-man crew, got into a 1,500 cwt truck and were driven out to our aircraft by a

WAAF. At the aircraft we were met by a couple of ground crew who presented us with a Form 700 – a maintenance record for the aircraft. They had ticked boxes on the form confirming that they'd carried out their checks and entered the amount of fuel loaded. I signed off the form and Ron and I climbed into the aircraft through the hatch below the cockpit. After I had been on the squadron for some time I was allocated my own aircraft, but for my first few trips I took what I was given, usually one of the older planes, which were readily identified because they were painted black rather than the camouflage of the newer types. The older planes tended to be a bit knocked around and a touch slower. In the main, 692 Squadron was flying the Mark XVI model of the Mosquito, which had only entered into service earlier in 1944, so we felt that we were flying with the most up-to-date version of one of the best aircraft of the war.

Inside the aircraft I plugged myself into the aircraft's radio and oxygen systems and carried out the pre-take-off checks. Like all aircraft the Mosquito had a trimming wheel to alter the trim of elevators and another for the rudder. I would see that these were working and that the settings were correct, then would adjust the propeller controls to ensure that they were delivering maximum power. Next, I would make certain that I was taking fuel from the correct tanks (the outboard tanks) and that they were full. Then a check that the flap settings were correct and that the supercharger switches were set at 'medium' –

when the aircraft reached 20,000 feet one switched the supercharger switch to 'high' so the superchargers blew a greater charge of petrol into the engine. Finally I would check that the radiator flaps were open to increase airflow, so that the engines did not overheat when taxiing on the ground.

It would take around two minutes to complete all of these routine checks, and after I confirmed that I had prepared the aircraft for take-off the Control Tower indicated that I was 'Clear to start', the instruction to fire up our engines. Then I signalled to the ground crew to remove the chocks and taxied to near the end of the runway where we lined up with the other aircraft. We did not fly in any sort of formation, we would just arrange ourselves along the perimeter track and then take off in sequence and proceed independently to the target. At the end of the runway there was a caravan with ground crew who were also in radio contact with the Control Tower. They would show each aircraft a green light, which was the signal to take off.

By this stage I was concentrating hard on my tasks and anxiety was not a problem, but while I waited for the green light, thoughts of what might go wrong passed quickly through my head and I would mentally rehearse what action to take. My Mosquito was heavily laden with a 4,000-lb bomb and a full load of fuel. If one of the aircraft's two engines failed during take-off, provided the aircraft had reached a safe flying speed, it could continue to climb on one engine, but only to a maximum height of 1,500 feet. The safe height for dropping a 4,000-lb bomb was 5,000 feet, so if this happened I would face an unattractive choice between releasing it at a low altitude and risk being blown up by my own bomb, or attempting to land overweight, with the danger that the aircraft's undercarriage would collapse and the bomb would go off.

On one of my early trips this happened to the aircraft directly ahead of me and the pilot found himself faced with exactly this dilemma. Immediately after he took off I heard him call that he'd lost an engine. Our aircraft was delayed for a few minutes and we then proceeded to take off ourselves, not knowing what had happened to the other aircraft. When we returned from the raid, after debriefing we went to breakfast and to our relief we were joined by the crew from the aircraft whose engine had failed. As they could only climb to 1,000 feet they had headed towards the Wash with the intention of dropping the bomb at sea and hoping to escape the blast at a low level. However, on their way to the Wash they saw an airfield with Drem lighting and decided instead to risk landing with the bomb aboard. Fortunately, their undercarriage held and the bomb did not detonate.

On another occasion, when Ron and I were not rostered on an operation, we were sitting in our Nissen hut while aircraft from the squadron left on a raid. We heard a squeal of tyres from an aircraft, followed by an enormous explosion. During a take-off with a crosswind a pilot had run his plane off the runway, the undercarriage had collapsed, and a fire started. The crew somehow managed to get out of the aircraft and run to safety – a difficult feat in a Mosquito because of the entry/exit beneath the fuselage – before the heat from the fire caused the bomb to explode. As the bomb had not properly detonated the explosion was relatively limited. If the bomb had fully detonated, our Nissen hut 300 yards away would have been blown to pieces, along with much of the base.

We shared our base at Graveley with 35 Path-finder Squadron, which was equipped with Lancasters. I heard a story that a year or so before my arrival a ground crew were winching a box of incendiaries into a Lancaster when the hoist broke; the box landed heavily, and the incendiaries started going off among the bombs. The ground crew ran for their lives and, to escape the subsequent detonations, somehow managed to clamber over the high barbed-wire fence that ran around the perimeter of the field. The explosions were so severe that freakishly a piece of propeller was blown a quarter of a mile across the airfield where it took off the arm of Gus Walker, the station commander at the time (and later an air marshal who ran the RAF rugby team). When the blasts eventually came to an end the ground crew tried to get back over the barbed wire, but without the adrenalin generated by the spur of running for their lives they found that they were unable to repeat their fence-hurdling exploits. Instead they had to return by walking some miles around the perimeter and coming in through the main entrance gate.

When the controller in the caravan gave the green light, I opened the throttle to take off. This needed to be done steadily; as the airspeed increased I had to concentrate on controlling the rudder to correct the Mosquito's tendency to swing to the left. The take-off speed was around 110–120 knots; when the aircraft reached this speed I eased back on the control column, the nose of the plane rose, and we lifted off the ground. We continued away at about 145 knots and climbed to cruising altitude.

We carried fuel in both outboard tanks and drop tanks. We used fuel from outboard tanks to take off and climb, and when we were established at cruising flight I told Ron to push the fuel transfer cocks to open the fuel lines from the drop tanks. This allowed air pressure to transfer fuel from the drop tanks into the outboard tanks, enabling us to dispense with the drop tanks if necessary in an emergency to increase the speed of the aircraft (normally we would return with the drop tanks).

Ron put me on course and tried to get a Gee fix every six minutes or so in order to check our route and find the wind speed and direction. We chatted on the progress of the flight, and with just the two of us the conversation would be relaxed and informal. We would concentrate on the business at hand, talking about the progress of the flight; the position of the other Mosquitoes from our squadron in the vicinity; whether we were picking up any ice; and other practical matters. On one raid, the engine was running roughly but it was still producing power and the temperature and oil pressure gauges seemed to be OK, so I decided to keep going to the target. When we returned, the mechanics said that they had to change the spark plugs but there was nothing seriously wrong.

I was a bit more gung-ho than Ron, who was more cautious. If something seemed to be going wrong, Ron would draw on his greater experience and say, 'Don't press on, the medal isn't worth it', and we'd laugh about it afterwards.

On all of the raids I went on we flew eastwards over the North Sea. Crossing the Dutch coast the anti-aircraft (AA) fire came up and the searchlights tried to locate us. Our aircraft would attract AA fire only when approaching a city or other defended area like the coastline. The AA bursts were an orange centre surrounded by a ragged and sinister-looking circle of black smoke. At the height we flew only the heaviest AA – the famous 88-mm-calibre guns and 107-mm guns – could reach us, and we were beyond the range of the pom-pom guns firing tracer up to a height of about 5,000 feet. In all my training I had been taught to fly as 'accurately' as possible, but on operations we were told to keep weaving all the time until the final run to the target, to avoid AA and enemy fighters. I wasn't all that apprehensive about AA, reasoning that the chances of being hit weren't high, especially in a Mosquito flying at 27,000 feet. If there was a moon or any light around, one would see balls of black smoke left by exploding anti-aircraft shells. I felt the jolt when the plane flew through the black smoke, but this was unavoidable. I don't recall a shell

92

bursting within 100 yards of our aircraft.

If AA exploded close by one could hear the sound of a dull thud, just as one could hear thunder in a thunderstorm. One couldn't hear any sound of bombs hitting the ground. The noise of the aircraft's engines dominated.

It was common to be momentarily exposed in a searchlight beam, and when over a defended target our aircraft was often caught in multiple beams and exposed for a minute or two, but we were flying at such a speed that we usually soon escaped the beams. The searchlights were mainly white, but some were bluish, and these were radar-controlled beams that continually swept across the sky. Once caught within the blue master light, other searchlights would be directed towards the plane. Normally, when flying at night the only light inside the cockpit was the faint glow from the instrument panel. If the aircraft was caught in a searchlight beam one was trained not to look out and risk being temporarily blinded and lose one's night vision. Instead the drill was for me to keep my head down and focus on looking at the instrumentation and taking evasive action, while Ron looked outside the aircraft and kept me informed of any threat from enemy fighters or AA.

If our flight path took us over heavy bomber targets, when looking down the fires started by the heavy bombers' incendiaries would be clearly visible. The fires were a vivid yellow and orange and seemed like an inferno of fire and explosions. They were an awe-inspiring sight but I don't recall thinking about how terrible it was for the people below; I was concentrating on our particular task, and the fires below were someone else's doing.

At our briefing we were given a track to run into the target to avoid chaos over the area with planes coming in from all directions and at risk of colliding. As I headed into the target I tried not to weave unless I was being ranged by ground radar. This final run in always felt very vulnerable, as Ron would be crouching in the nose looking through his bomb sight at the target indicator flares that had been dropped by Pathfinders, either directly on the target or, if there was cloud cover, in the sky above.[6] The colour of the flares varied in heavy bomber raids but in my experience we were usually bombing on red flares. As one approached the target one would see bomb blasts from the Mosquitoes immediately in front of us attacking the same objective. We did not carry incendiaries to start fires; the 4,000-lb bombs that we carried created an orange mushroom cloud when they exploded. In our aircraft at 27,000 feet we would not feel any shock wave from the blast below.

Once over the target Ron opened the bomb-bay doors and pushed the bomb release switch, saying 'Bombs gone.' To make sure that the bombs had actually gone (there had been instances where the bomb release had not worked and aircraft had returned with the bomb still on board) I pulled a lever on the side of the cockpit that operated the emergency bomb release. There was a significant jolt when the 4,000-lb bomb was liberated, similar to that experienced going through an AA

94

burst, and the aircraft immediately felt lighter and faster. We still had to stay on the bombing run course for the full minute that it took the bomb to reach the ground from the height of our aircraft, so that a photo recording where the bomb had landed could be automatically taken by a camera on the aircraft. Once the photo was obtained, Ron closed the bomb-bay doors and we got out on the prescribed route as fast as we could.

I relaxed slightly as the main danger now seemed behind us and we headed for home. However, on this first raid to Hamburg my knowledge of geography proved a bit lacking, as I inadvertently flew our aircraft directly over Heligoland, a small island in the North Sea 46 kilometres off the German coast, that was packed with anti-aircraft gun batteries. The flak quickly put paid to my complacency. I was forced to take evasive action and tried to put as much distance between our plane and the island as possible.

Once we got back within the range of Gee (which went about as far as the Ruhr) I put the nose of the aircraft down and sped back to our home aerodrome. From readings on the cathode tube in front of Ron he could identify Gee lines, which would lead us to the airfield. When we got close we could see the airfield lit up with lights; I lined the aircraft up with the gap in the lights that indicated the runway and we descended to it using the glide path indicator. If visibility was limited, we would descend to a safe height to make an approach using Standard Beam Approach (SBA). SBA worked within fifteen to twenty miles of the airfield and would guide the aircraft to the runway. Using SBA, one could take the plane down to about 200 feet.

I felt huge relief as our wheels touched down and I taxied the aircraft to the dispersal point. I thought that if other raids went like this then we'd be all right. Ron told me that what he'd been through before on Stirlings had been dreadful, and his spirits were also high after this relatively easy introduction to active service on Mosquitoes.

At the dispersal point we were greeted by the ground crew, the same group of three men who always looked after our Mosquito. I knew them by their first names; they were men in their thirties who always called me 'Sir', even though the RAF was relatively free of class divisions compared to the hierarchy of the Army. Like most aircrew, I formed a close bond with them; they were always pleased to see us when we returned safely, and grieved if an aircraft did not come back. I was conscious that my own father had been a mechanic during the First World War and he told me that I should try to be on good terms with the ground crew as I owed them a lot.

After exiting from our aircraft a truck drove us to the briefing room for a debriefing by the intelligence officer. He asked standard questions like: 'What time were you over the target?', 'What target indicators did you bomb on?', 'What was the weather like over the target?', 'What was the AA like?', 'Did you see any night fighters?'

I never actually saw a night fighter but frequently viewed the coloured flares used by them to mark the bombers' route. We had no defence against enemy fighters other than our speed, but at the time they did not seem to be a major concern. We reckoned we were faster than most German night fighters. I subsequently found out that the Germans had specially fuelled fighters specifically targeting Mosquitoes. We also knew that the Germans had jets but did not think that they flew at night.

Various other aircrew would arrive while this questioning was going on and when it was completed we would walk over to the Mess where all of us would have breakfast together. We had some Canadians on the squadron who found out that those going into action were entitled to a rum ration, and to humour this requirement the practice was to have a bottle of rum on the intelligence officer's desk. The Canadians particularly would avail themselves of this and get very exuberant. Our Nissen huts had metal pipes coming down from the roof, which served as chimneys for stoves, and once, as we were getting ready to go to bed after returning from a flight, they dropped Very cartridges down these pipes. The cartridges exploded, blew the lid off the stove and red-hot cinders from the stove ricocheted around the room as we all took evasive action. This was obviously the Canadians' way of letting off steam after surviving another mission. I never got this 'exuberant'; I just wanted to go to bed and get some sleep.

Chapter 10

On an Operational Squadron

From 28 August to 14 October 1944 Ron and I flew twelve further operations to Hamburg, Düsseldorf, Karlsruhe, Hanover, Bremen and Berlin. The return flights took between three and four hours, except for Berlin, which was just over four hours in duration. The high speed of the Mosquito made it a relative sprint compared to the marathon trips of the heavy bombers.

Berlin was the main target for 692 Squadron. Mosquitoes from the LNSF flew to Berlin for seventy consecutive nights. Nuremberg and the Ruhr were also viewed as tough targets, the latter because of its strong defences. By the time I arrived at the squadron, targets in France (which were generally regarded as slightly easier) were not available because most of France had been liberated. On the positive side, the Germans had lost their radar stations in France and Belgium and therefore no longer had the advance warning of raids that had previously enabled them to get their fighters airborne and in the right place.

Ron and I quickly became a good team. He was a very thoughtful, intelligent man and became expert at taking us to and from the target with minimum fuss. Coming back he would put us on a line on the Gee screen and we would go straight down the position line to intercept the SBA beam to the runway.[7]

Invariably we were told at our briefings that the objective for the operation was a railway marshalling yard or some other specific target; we weren't bombing cities indiscriminately. Our Mosquitoes carried 4,000-lb bombs that we were told would take roofs off houses 500 yards from the point of impact and our aim was to set free the bomb we carried within 500 yards of the exact target. When bombing we could see the bombs already dropped by other Mosquitoes ahead of us. The explosions of 4,000-lb bombs showed up as mushroom clouds – a little like those of atomic bombs. The day after a raid I always went to the squadron's photographic section and they would give me a copy of the photo of the blast from the bomb that we'd released. From the photo one could tell how well one had done by referring to the distance between the explosion and the target markers. I wanted to measure our performance, and also recognised the historic significance of what we were doing. I put these photos in my logbook, but when I recovered this book after the war I found that someone had removed them, presumably for security reasons.

The morality of my involvement in bombing did not hang over me; I was not troubled by what we were doing, although my preference would have been a defensive role. The attitudes of different airmen varied; most thought that the bombing campaign was something that we had to do to win the war, and their primary concern was their own survival. I did not discuss the issues with Ron but I knew that he was deeply affected by the awfulness of war. I suspect that this was not just his traumatic experience of flying in a Stirling squadron but also the thought of what was being done to the German cities. We were all volunteers and Ron was still prepared to fly with Bomber Command; any qualms were outweighed by his feeling that the job needed to be done.

A few days after I arrived, I was required to practise flying over East Anglia at night at 10,000 feet before diving down to 250 or 500 feet to fly along the Peterborough canal in order to rehearse dropping mines in the German canal system. This was called 'gardening practice'. I hadn't done such low-level flying before; it was normally prohibited because of the risks and complaints from the public. I found it difficult to stay at a precise speed and to slow down to the 195 knots required in order to drop the mines. I did a couple of practice flights and then eight aircraft from the squadron did the real mission to the Kiel canal in Germany. I was lucky not to be selected to go on this as we lost three or four of the aircraft that went. The boys who came back told me that the operation was extremely difficult because, as well as the usual anti-aircraft fire, the Germans had searchlights along the canal shining horizontally, to blind the attacking aircraft. The whole squadron was deeply affected by these losses, but there was no ceremony or pause, we just got on with our next operations.

With the British and American armies sweeping across France and into Belgium, by September 1944 we believed that the end of the war was near, and hoped it would all be over by Christmas. However, I do not think that this led anyone on the squadron to hold back or take less risks. I am not sure that this attitude was shared by all the armed forces, and suspect that the proximity of the end of the hostilities did have some effect on the commitment of units like the Guards Armoured Division when they failed to relieve the First Parachute Division, trying desperately to hold the bridge over the Rhine at Arnhem.

I never truly felt fear to any great degree, nor even particularly excitement on an operation. I didn't feel that I was bullet proof, but I was just fully occupied with the process of flying. I am sure that the shortness of most of the Mosquito's flights, and the need to be constantly engaged with the tasks of flying, meant that I did not face the same degree of fear as say a rear gunner on a heavy bomber, who would have been largely inactive for the majority of the flight and therefore have plenty of time to contemplate the risks of what they were doing. I knew that Ron was more anxious than I was as a result of his experience in Stirlings. There was no real feeling of terror flying over Occupied territory, though the dangers did concentrate the mind wonderfully.

As one purpose of the LNSF was diverting the night fighters from the main bomber attacks, we were not flying with the heavy bomber streams and I didn't see other planes being shot down while flying. Later, while on the ground in Holland, I observed a considerable number of Allied aircraft being shot down, and once I watched one Lancaster hit and collide with another, resulting in a colossal explosion as their bombs went off – all gut-wrenching sights. I never saw a dead body while I was serving with Bomber Command; instead the death of my fellow fliers was simply registered as a gap at the Mess table the next day.

We shared our Mess with 35 Squadron, which flew Lancasters. They tended to suffer heavier losses than us, and this may have made them a little more fatalistic. They certainly considered Mosquito pilots to be effeminate 'pansies' who did not have to face the music to the same extent as they did. With lower losses flying Mosquitoes the odds were in our favour and we expected to survive. I know that the heavy bomber crews tended to become obsessed about counting the missions towards the completion of their tour of operations; this wasn't such an issue for us.

When aircrew from the squadron went missing, a very businesslike procedure was set in train. The adjutant would cause the crews' personal possessions to be packed up, their bedding removed, families notified, and reports made to the Air Ministry. Life continued afterwards as it had before. There might have been a lot of alcohol drunk in the Mess afterwards, but there was no sort of church service or ceremony to mark the loss of the aircrew unless they died over England and there were bodies to bury.

I think that this was the right approach in the context and matched the British national character at the time, which did reflect a 'stiff upper lip' attitude towards stress and grief. While I consider that bottling up emotion is not helpful either, and have found talking about the darker aspects of my experiences important for dealing with them, it seems to me that most of us benefited from reining in emotion and avoiding sentimentality. When we turned the radio on in the Netherlands to listen to the BBC news, if Vera Lynn was singing one of her sloppy, sentimental songs we would switch it off – we preferred the more upbeat, stirring American songs like 'Yellow Rose of Texas'!

I was always impressed by the remarkable degree of technical sophistication on the part of both the British and Germans in the race to gain some advantage in the bombing war. As well as Gee and SBA we had a radar detector gadget called the 'boozer' aboard the plane. This consisted of two small radio receivers, one tuned to the German ground radar frequency and connected to an amber warning light, and the other tuned to the German night fighter frequency and connected to a red warning light.

Once over Germany the amber light went on dimly, and remained on, which told us that the aircraft was being watched by the German ground radar. As we were a diversionary force it was intended that our planes should be picked up by the German radar. If the amber light shone brightly that meant that our aircraft was being ranged from the ground for anti-aircraft fire and possibly for radar-directed searchlights. In either event, once the amber light came on brightly the procedure was to alter course to the left or right, usually by about 30 degrees, counting while waiting for shells fired at the aircraft to arrive (1 second per 1,000 feet of altitude, so if we were flying at 28,000 feet one would count to 28). It was possible then to see shells exploding where the aircraft would have been had it remained on course. After that it was a return to the original course. I had to take this evasive action on most missions that I flew, particularly raids to Berlin or other heavily defended points.

If the red warning light went on dimly it meant that an enemy night fighter was behind the aircraft somewhere. If the red warning light became bright then the drill was immediately to do the steepest, quickest turn, as then an enemy night fighter was immediately behind you and about to fire. Once, coming back across the North Sea, I heard a loud hissing noise in my headset. Afterwards I was debriefed by our intelligence officer as part of the usual routine and told him about this experience. He said that our radio frequency was close to the night-fighter's radar frequency and we had been listening to a German night fighter close by. This was somewhat disconcerting!

Chapter 11

On the Run

I was probably in a state of shock when I hit the ground, but in the forefront of my mind were the actions that I had been trained to perform if I was shot down, starting with burying the parachute. Quickly I undid my harness, disconnected my dinghy from my Mae West (in the plane I sat on the deflated dinghy), bundled the 'chute up with the dinghy then, leaving them in the field, walked to the edge in search of a suitable place to bury the various bits of aeronautical impedimenta.

The field was bordered by a fence running beside a shallow ditch, in which grew brambles and scattered bushes. The ground seemed soft, so I hurried back to my 'chute, picked it up together with the dinghy, carried the bundle to the ditch and dumped them in. A few minutes of scrabbling with my hands made a slight depression in the bank, under some rambling brambles. In went the parachute. Then ripping open the dinghy pack I felt for the food container. The first tin reached was a two-star red distress marine flare. Back it went. Then out came the ration tin and I put it into my pocket.

Swiftly the dinghy followed the 'chute into the hole, then in went my Mae West. Lastly I laid the dinghy pack over the hole as camouflage, following this with loose earth, clods of grass, even – to my regret – handfuls of nettles. After a few minutes nothing could be seen – in the night moonlight anyway – of the incriminating collection and off I scurried. From the time that I first found myself sitting in space, thoughts of escaping had been running through my mind. Natural instincts carried one through, supplemented by training. I never considered just surrendering to the Germans. If I had encountered a German soldier or policeman my attitude was that I would kill him rather than surrender. When first posted to the squadron we were given the option of carrying a pistol. The general advice was that aircrew should not carry weapons, but I was told that one should be aware that if shot down and surrounded by angry civilians one ran the risk of being lynched and might want to carry a gun to defend oneself. There was good evidence of British airmen being lynched and I had heard stories of Luftwaffe airmen being thrown into burning buildings by irate civilians during the London blitz. I chose not to carry a pistol with me and I don't remember anyone else on the squadron carrying a gun, but some American flyers did.

It didn't take more than a second or two to decide to make for Holland – only fifty miles away and with a far distant light like a setting sun to show me where the fighting was, from the shelling in the Arnhem/Nijmegen neighbourhood.

The light from the front seemed to be westwards from me, so to remove my presence from the scene of the crash and to avoid the logical decision to head directly towards the front, I set the Pole Star over my right eye and started off, heading to the north-west.

A narrow rutted farm track led away from my field and I proceeded with great caution, walking along its grassy verge. I could still hear dogs barking in the distance but then, suddenly, there came a sound that to me meant that the manhunt was on. It was the shrieking of a siren, combined with the noise of a car, apparently about two miles away to the north. I went on until, after about half a mile, my track merged into a lane, running about due north. So I took this lane, keeping under the shadow of the tall trees that lined each side. All this time I was looking for a straight road heading in a north-westerly direction.

After about a quarter of a mile this lane led into another at right angles and quite close to the corner there was a house, a lower window of which showed a light – at 1.40 a.m. in the morning! So into the hedge I went and through into the field beyond and then crept silently up to the hedge of this new road and looked across.

My first impression was that at the other side of the road there ran a canal, some 50 yards wide, but after careful scrutiny it turned out to be a very long, narrow field, covered with dew and shining whitely under the moon. So over the road I went and crawled on all fours across this field until I reached the far hedge. There I stopped and listened. To the north of me was considerable shouting and crashing about in a wood. I assumed that they were looking for me so I set off along my hedge but had only gone about 150 yards when the shouting increased. Lying down under the hedge, I pulled out my escape kit from the breast pocket of my battledress and started hunting for my compass and for the packet of energy pills. I could remember the intelligence man at Warboys saying, 'Take an energy tablet [Benzedrine] as soon as you hit the deck.' The compass I found easily as its luminous points showed up well. I even found a packet of white tablets in a cellophane packet and quickly took one. Then thrusting some Horlicks tablets in my pockets, lest I should lose the escape pack, I set off again.

The escape kit was standard issue and included barley sugars, a bar of chocolate, a needle and thread, a fishing line, razor and a bar of soap – everything in the kit tasted of soap. For most of the war escape kits also included a silk map and sum of money in local currencies. However, shortly before I was shot down there had been instances of aircraft landing at the recently liberated city of Brussels and airmen spending the money in their escape kits on living it up for a few days before returning to their units. As a result of this transgression the money and maps had been temporarily withdrawn from the kits. I cursed the absence of the money and maps, especially the latter, and felt great ill will towards the irresponsible airmen.

I could still hear men shouting in the distance which, added to the barking of dogs and the occasional wail of a siren, made life very eerie. Every shadow seemed to be a German, there appeared to be a German policeman behind every tree, so that sometimes I would stop for ten minutes at a time without moving, or come to a gateway and creep past on all fours. Once, while crawling across such a gap in a hedge, I mislaid my compass and spent some minutes groping in the grass in an endeavour to find it. Eventually I did and proceeded on with growing confidence as I realised that the darkness that seemed so threatening was in fact my friend in avoiding detection.

Then I came back on to a country lane and set off down this, passing a farmhouse on tiptoe and hiding behind the hedge for five minutes when I thought I saw a cycle light coming towards me. I even found a small wood that looked promising for a hiding place but the undergrowth proved too thick for me to fight my way through without creating the very devil of a noise. So I kept on down the road.

Then I heard shouting and what sounded like beating and new lights moving through a small wood, some half a mile ahead of me. I heard the sound of a heavy vehicle on the road behind me and beaters nearby. Initially I thought that the beaters were looking for me, but when I saw them with their torches I realised they were trying to avoid overhanging branches. It finally dawned on me that the shouting that I had heard was not a search party after me, but was connected to some other activity.

So waiting behind the hedge at the side of my wood until the beaters had worked well through it, I slipped in behind them, reasoning that a wood already searched, would not be scouted again, at least for some time. The vehicle slowly proceeded down the road and then turned off into the trees. Silhouettes showed against the flashes of torchlight and I could see that the truck was carrying something large, about the size of a Lancaster's fuselage. I had no idea what it was.

It was not long before I found a shallow weapon pit dug at the side of my wood – such a weapon pit as one found in England during the Home Guard days – covering a field of fire down the lane along which I had come, together with the field that ran beside it.

I lay in this shallow pit for some time, to rest and to watch. After a while the coast seemed to be clear so, cuddling up in the bottom, I struck a match under my coat to read the instructions on the packet of energy pills from which I had already taken one tablet. Only to find that the label said 'Water purifying tablets. One to each pint of water' – ugh! I then dug out the correct Benzedrine packet and took one for morale's sake.

It was not long, probably three-quarters of an hour, before the first signs of light began to appear in the east. As the dawn grew stronger I cast a critical eye over my wood and its surroundings, coming to the conclusion that my foxhole was no place to hide for a whole day. For one thing it was impossible to stretch one's legs when lying in the bottom and also, while the hedge at the extreme edge of the woodland hid me from view from the lane, there were only scattered trees between me and a path through the forest.

So standing up and moving with great caution I set off, creeping down this path. Having moved about 100 yards, I discerned a house ahead of me, situated on the opposite side of the wood from my foxhole.

It was now becoming daylight and I could better pick a good space in which to hide. About 10 yards from the edge of the wood and 30 yards from the house I came upon a shallow, but fairly dry, ditch, running parallel to the side of the forest. This looked admirable as the sides were well covered with brambles, sycamores, nettles and other camouflage, so into it I went.

Before I had settled in, some shouting not far away caused me to leave my ditch and crawl on hands and knees to the edge of the wood to reconnoitre. And a good job too! For in doing so I discovered that parallel to my ditch and some 7 yards distant there was a path, which of course meant that anyone lying in the nearby ditch would have to be on his guard. At the perimeter of the wood I lay and surveyed the view below. Far from me a field sloped away down to a wooded valley. In this field a girl of about eighteen and a boy perhaps ten were herding cows towards the nearby farmhouse for milking. So returning to my ditch once more I started to make myself comfortable. The bottom was slightly damp, but by collecting all the small twigs close at hand I was able to make a small wooden carpet big enough to keep my hip and elbows dry while I lay down.

I took stock of my situation. I had been knocked about and bruised but nothing was broken. My eyebrows were split and I had bitten through my lip. Then there was the question of uniform. My battledress, by daylight, was indeed in poor shape. The left sleeve had been practically severed at the

111

shoulder and had a long rent in it below the elbow. My trousers were torn at the knees and had sundry small rips. And of course I still had my various badges identifying me as an RAF airman.

In the top of my 'escape boots' there was a tiny pocket that was meant to contain a small penknife to cut the top off the boots. A search for the penknife drew a blank – it must have fallen out of the pocket into space during my descent. So for the purpose of removing my wings, name tag and rank ribbons, the razor blade from my escape kit had to be used. Off they all came, to be buried in the bank of my ditch. Similar treatment was applied to my flying boots, and the razor blade quickly took off the tops, leaving the escaping shoes. The lambskin from the tops made splendid cushions for my hips and bottom respectively.

Then I tried to sleep but it was difficult. Up until then I was preoccupied with my own survival, but then came a time for reflection on what had happened, and why, and what fate had befallen my good friend Ron. I was bowed down with worry about him. At the time we were hit he had already crawled down into the nose to set the wind strength and direction on the bomb sight. His parachute pack, meanwhile, was in a stowage just in front of where he normally sat beside me. With the wild gyrations of the aircraft when it started to disintegrate, was there any chance of him reaching his parachute and clipping it on as I was flung out? The chances were virtually nil and the outcome almost too grim to contemplate.

Then there were thoughts about my own family. How would they react after receiving the inevitable telegram – missing in action? How would my girlfriend Pam get the news? I felt crushed by the magnitude of the tragedy.

At 9 a.m. a Focke-Wulf (FW) 190 flew low round the wood at great speed and at 10 a.m. I heard the diesel engine of a large vehicle start up. Soon afterwards, and with an earth-shattering roar, a V2 rocket took to the air, close by. This explained the shouting, beating and lights of the previous night – I had landed near a mobile V2 launcher. As at 15 October 1944 no official mention had ever been made to the effect that V2s were in fact being used. There had been rumours about them and I knew of their existence from intelligence briefings reporting that bomber crews had seen smoke trails going up into the sky that they couldn't account for. It was not until later that Churchill officially announced that the Germans were firing rockets and there was no means of advance warning. And there was I within a few hundred yards of one. The whole idea of rockets seemed utterly fantastic to me, an extraordinary thing that had not even been contemplated when I was a boy.

In the course of the morning three rockets were fired, each time after a reconnaissance flight by the FW190. At the time I assumed that the rockets were being launched against London, but later I found out that these rockets were being fired at the port of Antwerp. Antwerp had been captured on 4 September 1944 with its port facilities almost intact, and it was vital that it be re-opened as a supply port for the Allied armies in the Netherlands and northern Germany. The German-held approaches to the Scheldt river needed to be liberated first, and it took until 28 November 1944 for Antwerp to be re-opened. In the meantime the Germans started range-finding launches on 7 October and the first V2s landed in Antwerp on 13 October 1944, only two days before I saw the three rockets fired on the morning of 15 October 1944. The mobile launcher I was observing was one of a battery of launchers concealed in the countryside around Münster. The V2 bombardment of Antwerp continued until 27 March 1945 and during this period more than 1,600 rockets fell on Antwerp. I knew none of this at the time but it was clear to me that this was a significant development in the war and I was determined to get back to England to report that the Germans were firing V2s from mobile sites. When I reached Holland five days later, I witnessed columns of white smoke, almost daily, rising vertically into the sky some ten miles to the east in Germany, these being the tell-tale signs of the launch of rockets. I noticed perhaps three or four launches in a day, suggesting that the firing line had moved westwards. Frequently there were huge explosions soon after launch indicating a high failure rate.

The morning's breakfast was frugal to say the least, consisting of one boiled sweet and a few Horlicks tablets. These tablets in particular were phenomenally hard and took almost ten minutes to eat. On top of that, they and everything else in the pack tasted of soap, or rubber from the rubber water bag also contained in the kit.

The only other excitement during the morning occurred when a middle-aged lady dressed in black and wearing a conical witch-like hat, sailed along the nearby path on her bicycle.

Lunch was similar to breakfast – the two blocks of coconut-toffee stuff being reserved for my 'operational meal' to be eaten before walking, it being the only food with any bulk in the escape pack.

During the afternoon some children came and played in the wood, bringing with them a small dog. From that moment onward I was quite convinced that if anything or anyone proved to be my downfall, it would be small children or dogs!

The only other people who put in an appearance during the day were two ladies, one of them wearing a most expensive fur coat, who walked up to the nearby farm in the afternoon and returned later in the day.

Outside the farm were two very fine cars – Mercedes V8s I thought, which gave me the idea that the wealthy business people from the Ruhr lived in these outlying districts and drove into work in the daytime. Pure speculation.

At about six in the evening I started to make ready for the road. It was beginning to get dark now and the time seemed ripe. I tried to put the two lambskin tops from my flying boots inside my battledress blouse but there was no room for two, so one had to suffice, and I put it into the front. I had my operational meal and consumed two lumps of my coconut toffee.

Then, just as things seemed about right for

departing, it started to rain. There did not appear to be anything that could be done about it so off I went, walking along the nearby path and heading northwards through the wood. Soon the track left the trees and struck off across two meadows, converging on a main road. It was still fairly light and, just where my path met this main road, there was a signboard. But there were also a few scattered houses on both sides of the road, not to mention a few people about, so I decided not to attract attention to myself by walking over to study it and instead set off straight down the road.

Two small children were ahead of me and these were soon overtaken, but as I passed they accelerated, asking me, apparently, to walk down the road with them as they were afraid of the planes, should they come. 'Little bastards,' I thought (rather uncharitably) and pressed on. But the faster I walked, the faster they ran. Until we were all flying along at a great pace.

However, my endurance seemed a little better than theirs so that I beat them into the nearby village. A uniformed laddie whom I took to be a policeman stared rather hard at me as I walked through, while two pairs of eyes peered inquisitively from an upper window, but there were no complications. Soon I turned left and walked westwards for the best part of a mile before the road turned into a farm track and started to veer back towards the village again. So there was nothing to do but start out across country, which I did, but the going was hard and the first field I struck was nearly ankle deep in water. And still it drizzled with rain! Then I was confronted with a river running across my path. Not a big river, admittedly, but to me it constituted an 'impasse' – one of my self-imposed regulations being that I should keep as dry as was possible. So I struck off southwards along the bank of the 'impasse' until after much squelching through the mud I came to a small rickety bridge, which led me past a farmhouse and on to a main road heading south-west.

All these compass headings may sound irksome but it must be remembered that the only means of getting from one place to another was to make a guess at its direction and steer that course with my little ½-inch compass. I was still looking for a road heading in a north-westerly direction.

By now it was dark and drizzling intermittently, while the road stretched away before me – dead straight for many miles.

One occasionally passed the odd farm standing well back from the road and showing small chinks of light through the blackout. The German blackout seemed to be nothing like as strict as ours. The only large building close to the road that I came across for some miles was an inn from which exuded the most delicious smell of cooking – made more enticing by my hunger. Various men passed me on bicycles but only one of them spoke to me. Instead of maintaining a stony silence, like a clot I said 'Guten Abend', which produced some question from my comrade on the road to which I could only make some inarticulate reply. However, after a moment of uncertainty, he pulled off into the darkness.

Suddenly a German voice boomed out right

beside me. I had almost walked into a German bending down at the roadside, trying to get his bike lamp to work, and it seemed that he thought that I might have a match. So I fumbled in my pocket in an attempt to find a match, but before one could be produced another man rode up behind us on a bike and brought his lamp on the scene. Whereupon I quietly slid away.

About this time I started to hear the most extraordinary massed chorus. It started with a man's voice singing a clear refrain, then hundreds of voices taking up the same refrain.[8] It seemed to come from some distance away, yet never appeared to get nearer or further away, and I later discovered that parallel to the main road down which I was walking there ran a railway line, where trains were stopped, owing to the presence of 'intruder aircraft' overhead. So while sitting in the darkness inside them, the people sang. At the time I thought that the singers were German troops, but I now believe it is likely that they were Jews or other prisoners on their way to concentration camps.

Eventually I came to a bridge that carried the main road across the railway line, but having been travelling south-west all this while, I decided it was about time that a strike was made to the west. So instead of crossing the bridge, I headed off along a country lane in the direction of the red glow that marked the front.

By 3 a.m. I was so tired that I could hardly stagger along the road, so coming into a small town or large village I tried all the doors of the church, hoping that I might find a refuge there, but they were locked and I had to seek shelter elsewhere. Having walked right through this settlement, I struck out across some fields towards a wood and in this I tried to rest and shelter. But the rain came on harder than ever and after about a quarter of an hour I got up and stumbled off in search of something better.

Reaching a farmhouse I tried the barn door without success and was just about to hunt around further when in the darkness my eyes lighted upon what appeared to be the entrance to an air-raid shelter and in I went. Technically it was an air-raid shelter, but it had not been used as such for a long time, its more recent occupants having been chickens, which left the air in there tainted with a particularly poultry odour. But it was dry and the wind was kept on the outside.

So taking off my wet shoes and hanging up my soaking battledress, I pillowed my head on my lambskin boot top and fell asleep.

The noise of farm work awoke me at about nine in the morning and, looking cautiously through the entrance of my retreat, I could watch the comings and goings of the farm people. One lad in particular spent most of the day carting mangelwurzels[9] into the barn. Each time he passed, I felt that his horse knew of my presence as it turned its head towards the air-raid shelter, though fortunately the yachting-capped lad on the cart did not.

I reflected on my situation and concluded that I would have to keep on walking until: (a) I knew I was in Holland through crossing a definite frontier; (b) until I reached the front; or (c) until

I could see at least three windmills at one time.

And still there was the nightmarish, ever-present worry as to what Ron's fate had been. Perhaps he had managed to get to his parachute and was now a prisoner, or perhaps he never did get his 'chute on at all, in which case it must have taken him nearly three minutes to fall to his death, poor chap!

The day passed slowly. I had my 'meals' at regular times and watched what little I could of the outside world passing by. Thirst was becoming the major problem.

Towards evening a very muscular girl appeared, pushing a large wheelbarrow full of mangel-wurzels and then peace descended upon the place. The working day was done.

Being so close to the farmhouse it was necessary to wait until complete darkness fell before continuing the journey and when I did emerge into the fresh air, it was to discover that I was not certain of the path back to the main road. So striking out along the most definite cart track I could find, I soon found myself trudging through the last village I had passed the night before. And again I could smell cooking...

The blackout of this place would have been a paradise for an officious British Bobby – not only were there quite considerable chunks of light showing, but in some cases one could actually see into the rooms from which light came.

After clumping down the cobbled streets I shortly came out into the main road, quite close to the church whose doors I had tested the previous night, and off I set westwards again.

It was now my third night on German soil and, while feeling somewhat peckish, I also felt decidedly thirsty. It was, of course, raining substantially and just walking with my mouth open helped things considerably, but just the same I longed for the sight of some source of water.

The night grew darker and darker as I walked, until the only guide to the direction of the road lay in the narrow gap in the trees that could just be discerned overhead. And then I heard the wonderful sound of running water. Not the drip and gurgle of water sliding down the tree trunks, nor the squelch of my own boots even, but real running water. At first I could not see where it came from but I soon discovered that I was standing on a small bridge over a stream about 4 yards wide. Eagerly I slipped round the edge of the parapet and nearly took a header down the almost vertical bank, which stood some 4 feet above the water. Not wanting to get any wetter than I was, the only alternative was a gymnastic feat, hanging from one of the girders of the bridge with one hand while scooping a little water up in my forage cap with the other. This proved very satisfactory, except for the fact that each scoop of the hat only produced about a gill of water, my anthropoidal arms not being quite anthropoidal enough.

Before I had had time for more than about four scoops, I became conscious of a very heavy rumble, which seemed to be getting nearer. So pausing in my operation I scrambled back to the top of the bridge. Soon long beams of light could be seen approaching along the road, going in the same direction as myself. Then, crouching behind the parapet of this little bridge, I saw ten of the largest Army lorries that I have ever seen, go rolling by. Every one being a six-wheel diesel, with each wheel at least 4 feet in diameter. I reckoned that a single lorry could carry a platoon and so about a full battalion was passing. I could hear the singing of the men and could just discern large branches of foliage draped over the roofs of the lorries by way of camouflage. And I was needlessly frightened – needlessly because even had they seen a solitary figure trudging down the road, long after curfew, I'm sure that they would not have stopped any of the lorries to investigate the situation.

Once they had travelled on, off came my cap again, into the water it scooped, down my throat went the last drops of water, and off I headed again!

The next excitement came when I discovered a large square signboard standing upright on the ground at the right-hand side of the road. I was just about to strike a match to read the sign when I heard another lorry coming, so nipping to the western side of this board, I sat down with my back against it, hoping that the lorry coming from the east would shoot past without even a glimpse of me crouching down.

This strategy worked out splendidly, the only snag being that having passed me, the lorry stopped some 30 yards down the road and the driver hopped out armed with a torch and came back to read the signboard. I had the presence of mind to nip round to the side of my signboard away from my chum with the light, but also had the nasty feeling of not quite knowing what to do next. But I watched the proceedings with interest.

The German waved his torch to and fro as he advanced and when about 10 yards from me directed its beam on another signboard, which I had not as yet observed. This seemed to satisfy him for he then turned about, climbed aboard his lorry and rumbled off into the darkness.

Once my nerve was restored, I too set about reading these signboards. All the information the board that I had hidden behind could provide was 'A1' written in letters 2 feet high. The other, by the light of two of my precious matches, said 'AHAUS' to the right and 'WINTERSWIJK' to the left – neither of these names conveying anything to me. But at the crossroads 50 yards further on down the road, it became apparent that the Ahaus road headed north-westwards, while the Winterswijk road ran almost due west. So this latter road, leading, as it seemed, straight towards the front at Arnhem, became my line of flight.

It had been raining pretty steadily all the evening and while it left me damp, dripping and mortally cold, it was that very cold that kept me on the move, kept other people off the road, and shielded me with the cloak of darkness.

Time passed slowly and my feet became very sore, particularly my right foot. The lambswool lining of my boots was causing rubbing against the skin owing to the wool pilling. At the end of my walk a large piece of the skin of my feet peeled away like a rasher of bacon.

Just before midnight, during a fairly heavy shower, I came through a village or hamlet, still showing chinks of light through the windows of the houses. Nobody seemed disposed to come out into the cold to question the presence of one dishevelled traveller and he did not feel disposed to enquire as to his whereabouts.

I had just reached the last house in the hamlet when I nearly walked into a barrier across the road that I had not noticed in the darkness, so slipping into the hedge I considered the situation. Two German soldiers stood in a sentry box at the end of this barrier and snatches of their conversation were borne downwind to me. They seemed to think much the same about the weather as I did.

From the main road upon which I had been travelling a small rutted lane seemed to branch off to the left, parallel to the barrier. A detour of this barrier was obviously necessary and while I could not climb through the hedge beside me, there seemed no reason why I should not walk up to the barrier, turn left down this lane and, when out of the view of the guards, nip across the fields and back on to the road again. This I did, marching up to the barrier and turning left just 5 yards from the sentries. If they saw me – and they must have done so – they probably concluded that I was a German soldier returning from midnight revelries.

The field picked as a short cut was ploughed, making the going fairly heavy and, as I crossed it, first a car came down the road, pausing at the barrier, and then some heavy lorries, doing likewise. Then I was back on the road heading westwards.

My right foot was feeling terribly raw and it was necessary to limp along, keeping my weight off it – all of which made the time drag and the distance seem immeasurable. But at length I found I was passing houses again. As I proceeded, the buildings became more concentrated until they lined both sides of the street and I knew that I was entering a town. The metalled road turned into cobblestones and the noise of my iron-shod heels became deafening as it reverberated through the empty streets.

Shops started appearing, making it evident that this was the main street. Very few chinks of light showed; all was silent as the grave – apart from my seemingly deafening footsteps. Again delicious smells could be sniffed – sweet buttery smells, oniony smells, smells which brought visions of steaks and fried eggs and bacon – all of which accentuated my hunger and thirst to an unbearable degree.

It now occurred to me that it was perhaps foolish to pass through the main street raising all hell with the noise of my boots. Having passed a German sentry outside the town hall, I decided to take a turning to the right and seek a quieter, or rather a less central, road.

So I turned right and in less time than it takes to tell I found myself marching straight for a party of four or five Germans who were walking my way, laughing and joking as they came.

I assumed that I had been seen and thought that my best strategy was to impersonate a German soldier, so with a tremendous Initial Training Wing (ITW) crash I came to an ITW halt and did an ITW 'about turn' right in the middle of the road. Then I marched off back into the main street again.

A bit further along I found another street turning to the right, which in turn changed into a suburban road apparently running parallel to the main street.

Some of the houses in this road appeared to be missing roofs. I had not passed more than two or three houses in this condition when, crash! I fell slap on my chest into a large bomb crater right in the middle of the road. There was also a rather unpleasant smell of gas too.

While picking myself up I wondered what these battered houses would be like to live in and whether there might be some food. But the smell of gas, and the likelihood of workmen in the day-time, put me off.

Although the fall had not hurt me in any way, it had brought to mind the fact that I was becoming increasingly fatigued. My feet seemed to be swinging forward more by their own momentum than by any strength of mine, and this blasted right foot pained me considerably.

Several more missing roofs were passed before the end of the road was reached – and here the reason for the bombing was apparent, for two railway tracks converged and then ran in parallel at the level crossing at the road's end. Many bomb holes could be seen close to the rails, but to all intents and purposes there had not been one direct hit.

There the road deteriorated into a cart track leading through a wood and 'wallop', once again I tripped over some obstacle in my path and fell full length in the road. This time it was a fallen tree and a closer examination showed various other trees uprooted or torn off close to the ground – more bombs had fallen here, some 400 yards from the railway.

While still in the wood I came upon a fork in the track and, taking the one to the right, soon found myself walking across a wooden bridge that made a dull, hollow, reverberating sound at every cautious footfall. There must have been a farmhouse some 50 yards past this bridge, though it remained invisible in the trees and gloom, and a dog suddenly commenced barking furiously. I stopped to see whether it would quieten down but, no, it was obviously suspicious and continued to bark until a man's voice shouted to it. When the barking carried on, the man then stumbled from the house, and his tramping could be heard coming down the lane. I quickly retraced my steps, tiptoeing across the bridge and taking the left-hand branch of the fork in the lane. There I sped away as quickly as my feet would carry me – which wasn't much at that!

The going was much harder down this lane and after twenty minutes or so I had to stop and rest. As my throat was dry beyond belief, I had to search round for some source of water. Although it was still drizzling, and all the trees and bushes dripped and gurgled with the abundance of dampness, there was no still limpid pool. One might have been in the Sahara! Then my eyes lighted on the ruts in the lane itself; they at least had collected puddles of water – water for which I was dying. So carefully removing the lid from my escape kit, I dipped it into the puddle and drank perhaps a wineglass full. It was muddy and tasted slightly of horse dung, but it was water and though I may not have drunk it with relish, it went down with a certain satisfaction. In fact I had a second lidful and then a third before carefully packing up my things and continuing on my way.

Half a mile further on and the lane led through the yard of another farm and, with memories of the recent dog episode, a wide detour seemed sensible, so taking to the fields I attempted to walk round the farm and return to the lane. But after making a circuit of about a quarter of a mile, I found myself cut off by a 10-foot-wide stream. Although on my first night's walking a 10-foot stream could have easily been cleared with a short run, on this, the third night, the effort required seemed rather too great.

Returning to the lane I then proceeded initially to walk through the farmyard, and then through a second farmyard, and in passing the second was bold enough to try all the doors of the barn in search of a resting place for the morrow. But no luck.

A little later it came on to rain rather hard, and though flashes of gunfire could still be seen in the far distance, I seemed to be drawing no nearer to that ultimate goal, the front. So, cold and discouraged, I tried to dig into the side of one of a small collection of small, round, pointed haystacks. The straw was old and stiff and I could not work myself in. A short snack in the shelter nevertheless served to build up my morale a little.

A canal was the next permanent landmark, and walking along its bank I soon came upon a disused fowlhouse with thick filth on the floor and not much of an excuse for a roof. Though hardly in a position to be fussy I thought I could find better shelter than that.

I did – though not for about another hour, in which time I had crossed the canal by a narrow iron bridge, walked down a main road, passed by a number of houses and finally trekked beyond a railway station in a large village. There the road terminated in a 'T' junction, with the road to the left leading apparently southwards while the one to the right led north.

I took the one to the right and followed it beside the same canal for some two miles. Then it left the canal and ran between banks with an occasional peak in them where paths and tracks led off to the surrounding farms. Then – joy of joys – right opposite a farmhouse and cut deep into the bank, was what appeared to be an air-raid shelter.

Closer examination revealed that it really was an air-raid shelter and furthermore was admirable for my purpose. It ran along inside the bank with its roof supported with beams on pit props. There was a bench of sorts upon which to sit and, most important of all, there was a second entrance (or exit) on to the field side of the bank at the opposite end to the road entrance. That meant that if anyone popped their head in, I should stand a fair chance of nipping out at the rear and still remaining unobserved from the road.

It was then about 4 a.m. and as the cocks began to crow I lay down, fully dressed and soaked to the skin, and within five minutes was sound asleep.

At about 9 a.m. I awakened, shivering with the cold, and endeavoured to beat my arms to circulate the blood. It brought a little temporary relief, but the wind blew in through the back door, whistled through my sopping clothes, and then expelled itself through my front door.

By sitting well inside I could look out and watch the passers-by, confident that the darkness within hid me sufficiently. Farmers going to their fields trudged along. Schoolchildren skipped past. The postman walked by. A farm cart rumbled onwards, driven by a German soldier in a grey uniform, with another soldier similarly clad lying in the back chewing a straw. A glimpse of this fellow's face filled me with confusion, for in place of his right eye he had a black patch – a most piratical patch – and this being my first daylight glimpse of a German soldier, I was moved to speculate what the remainder looked like. Little did I know! I was told later that wounded German soldiers would be sent home to help work on farms, which perhaps explains the presence of the one-eyed soldier on the cart.

During the day I had two anxious moments, once again caused by those arch menaces to an evader's safety – small children and dogs. The dogs came first – two of them with an old chap wearing a yachting cap, who seemed to gain more propulsion from his walking stick than he did from his legs. But those damned dogs! They came snuffling up to the entrance of my hideout. I'm not very good with dogs at the best of times, having been bitten when I was young, and felt quite convinced that if they smelt my presence they would crouch outside snarling and barking. Fortunately the old man was unwittingly on my side and called them to heel just as the danger was becoming apparent.

Shortly afterwards some small children came up the road with a dog. Once again the dog sniffed around the entrance to my hideout until the children called it away.

The hours passed slowly and the cold was penetrating. My wet clothes merely seemed to lower the temperature of an already icy blast. All day long I rubbed my hands together, beat my legs and thought of large meals in dry, warm rooms.

At last the sun began to sink. My impatience to be off was so great that before it was anywhere near dark, I set off up the road, finding my legs very weak and wobbly after sitting cramped up for fourteen hours. But soon the circulation returned and with it came warmth and confidence.

When two bicycle lights approached I hid in the bushes beside the road and waited for them to pass – but when ten minutes had gone by and they had not reached me, it dawned on even my intelligence that they must have turned off somewhere. So I stepped back into the road once more – and found myself face to face with a German soldier who was walking quietly down the highway. He looked at me and I looked at him. There was nothing to do but walk on, look as unconcerned as possible, and hope that my uniform and forage cap looked sufficiently innocuous in the half light and that he took my presence in an isolated hedge to be the answer of a call of nature.

A certain warmth on the back of my neck told me that he stood and watched as I retreated up the road, but evidently he was not sufficiently suspicious to take any further action.

Soon I came to a major junction and paused to read the signboard. It was now just too dark to distinguish the lettering so I endeavoured to strike a match. No luck. Then just as I was taking out a second match I heard footsteps behind me, so pocketing my matches set off without further ado. A native does not usually have to pause near his village to read signboards! It seemed that the footsteps were keeping pace with mine. At all costs they must not catch me and start a conversation, I thought, and soon was galloping along at a cracking pace. Still the footsteps kept up! So there seemed to be nothing to do but to turn up the first side road and hope that 'footsteps' – our chum – kept heading straight on. I turned off and he kept going. Cheers!

Then it started to rain and the wind, already strong, blew harder and harder. Thrusting down the road the effort became greater and greater. Many times I stopped for shelter or rest under trees and bushes but it was no use. Then came a great road junction with a conspicuously fine signboard, one arm of it pointing to a place named 'DOETINCHEM'. It sounded Dutch. Could it be I wondered? Had I really crossed the frontier? Should I now try to get some more assistance? These thoughts ran through my head as I turned in the direction of Doetinchem. I dared not try for help – I must reach the front.

The rain was teeming down now and the wind blowing hard in my teeth, making the going indescribably hard. I passed a huge water tower.

The rain was unyielding and my vision so limited, that when I saw a flashlight waving a hundred yards ahead of me I continued towards it, resolving not to take evasive action until close to it. And thus it was that I almost walked right into the behinds of two gentlemen of the Wehrmacht bending over the radiator of their broken-down lorry parked at the side of the road with its lights off. They obviously did not hear me in that screaming wind, even as I had not heard them, so stepping off the road I stood behind a tree some 5 yards from the Germans. One was singing 'Mein Vader is ein Gadagen', which I guessed meant 'My father is a garage worker' or something similar, and thought it very funny under the circumstances – and who says that the Germans have no sense of humour? Seldom have I seen such rain. One man kept waving his torch about so I quietly sneaked from my tree and over the barbed-wire fence intending to head into the open road. No sooner was I on the far side of the fence than two headlights turned full on to me. I dropped flat in that soaking grass and prayed.

133

Two trucks were parked behind the broken-down one and evidently despairing of moving the latter before daybreak, the other two switched on their lights, started up and drove up a small turning some 10 yards further up the road – I had climbed over the fence almost on the corner of this road. As each light passed over my body I froze internally – but no surprised shouts came; after all, it was a beastly night and they would not have been looking across the fields for cowering escapees.

Soon afterwards, the struggle seemed too great and I tried the door of a henhouse that I reached by walking past the back door of a farmhouse. No luck.

Another mile or so down the road and another attempt to open a barn door. It would not budge either. But I had to get in. I was soaking. I had not eaten for five days. I had had only one real drink – out of my hat from a muddy stream – and I was dead beat with the wind and rain and sodden clothes, not to mention waterlogged shoes, which felt like they weighed a ton, and a right foot seemingly on fire.

Feeling along the wall past the big barn doors, I touched a smaller door and with a tug it opened! Inside it was pitch black – it was completely dark outside for that matter but this was even more impenetrably black – and there was that dry musty smell of hay. It smelt warm and inviting to a deadbeat. It also seemed quiet and safe enough to strike a match – and I found I was in a tiny room surrounded by back-to-back brooms, spades, old sacks and all kinds of farm junk.

This room had a wooden wall 6 feet high, with no ceiling. High above appeared to be the hayloft, with a ladder leading up to it.

And such proved to be the case when I climbed up. In fact, the hayloft itself was less than half full, the main pile of straw being at one end. For the first time I took off my soaking clothes and in a far and deserted corner hung them up to dry. Then I went back to the straw pile where, after a moment of digging and worming deep into that warm inviting straw, I fell into a sound, dreamless sleep. It was about 3 a.m.

Chapter 12

Discovery

There are no doubt many methods of joining partisans, but one that can be highly recommended is that of seeking a barn beside a farmhouse in an 'enemy-occupied' country, leaving your trousers in an inaccessible corner (inaccessible to you at least!), digging into the straw in another part, and falling asleep. It may also help if one has two black eyes, a fair amount of clotted blood on one's person, and a week's growth of beard. That at least was the setting for my initiation.

My sleep was as sound and dreamless as only the sleep of starvation and exhaustion can be. Nothing short of an earthquake could have awakened me – and as I regained consciousness with a start, it was with the thought that an earth-quake was indeed taking place. With a shrieking, crackling roar something seized my barn by its four corners and shook it, so that the dust filtered through the floor of the loft. Quickly I advanced to the wooden weatherboards of the barn wall and peered through a crack. On the road, 50 yards from my barn, stood the smoking remains of a car and the howl of a Rolls-Royce Merlin engine made itself apparent. This brought an overwhelming desire to bury myself in the straw – completely ineffectual against cannon-fire though it was. Which I did. As the Spitfire came down the engine's howl was punctuated first by the bass thudding of cannon, then by the crackling hiss of small-bore machine guns. Then he was up and away. My heart was beating fast and my palms were damp but there seemed to be no holes in my person. Scarcely had the sigh of relief died, when my breathing stopped al-together. Someone had tiptoed into the barn. It did not take a second to submerge completely into the straw, but my heartbeats seemed to reverberate round the barn and my breathing remained in a state of permanent inhalation. The tiptoeing receded with my exhalation.

Mutterings against the singular lack of tran-quillity in rural Europe likewise froze on my lips as more footsteps approached and this time they hardly tiptoed. They hurried and there seemed to be two pairs of feet. A whispered consultation was held close by – then cautious footsteps up the ladder leading to the loft came to my ears. My trousers! Would they find my most valuable garments in the loft? Apparently all was well, for having retired to a corner there was silence. Who were these people, though, and from whom were they hiding? The feeling that they must be friends was strong but I could not be sure.

Suddenly an exclamation from above reached me, then excited whisperings, then quite distinctly I heard a voice saying 'ROYAL AIR FORCE', as if reading. My clothes! I jumped out from the straw and there before me were two youths of sixteen or seventeen years of age holding my precious garments. They looked at me in amazement – I am not shown off to my best in a pair of underpants.

One of the lads quickly recovered and in halting English said, 'You are English?'

'Yes,' I replied. 'Am I in Holland – where is this place?'

'Be "still",'[10] he replied. 'There are two Germans from that car in the farm-house. You are in Aalten, 5 kilometres in Holland from the German frontier.' I was among friends and a great handshaking ensued.

After restoring their confidence in a German victory with copious draughts of Dutch ersatz coffee, the Germans departed from the farm-house. Plans were then laid for my future existence. The boys were afraid of telling the farmer – the father of the elder boy – about me as they said he was 'nervous', but they promised to bring me food and drink – which they did – great chunks of dry bread upon which were laid thin slices of raw bacon and thin slices of black bread. And they brought a cup of milk. Thirst was the real craving and the milk consequently disappeared in a flash. Please could I have some water? More milk. Water please? More milk, and so on. Then they left me to sleep, with a small hoard of delicious apples to chew when I felt so inclined, and saying that they would investigate the possibility of contacting the Underground!

That evening I was awakened by the whole family Breukelaar – the boys having decided to tell them all. Mother, Father, Grandmother Breukelaar, their daughter, a pretty child of about fifteen years, and their son. They came by candlelight and all shook hands with this bedraggled creature who hid in their strawpile.

We laughed and chattered as I ate the food they brought – the translation being done by the elder boy, who it transpired was wanted for work in Germany in the 'Arbeitsdienst'.

'When will the Tommies liberate Holland?'

'Before the New Year – Churchill has promised,' I replied – rather optimistically as it turned out.

'Have you ever bombed Holland?'

'No!'

'Have you ever heard of the NSB or Seyss-Inquart?'

'No I haven't.' Little did I know what significance NSB (the Dutch Nazi Party) and Seyss-Inquart (the Governor of Holland) had in store for me. Together they represented all the terror, hatred and misery in Holland.

The NSB was the Nationaal-Socialistiche Beweging in Nederland – the Dutch Nazi Party. Like many far right political parties it had attracted some minority support during the depression years of the 1930s although this popular support had declined by the time of the German invasion in May 1940. My Dutch friends blamed the malign influence of the NSB for reducing Dutch resistance to the German invasion to a brief five days of confused fighting. Under the German occupation the NSB was left as the only legal political party and enthusiastically collaborated with the occupying forces, undertaking such unsavoury tasks as rounding up Jews and the Arbeitseinsatz – the drafting of civilians for forced labour. By the time I arrived in the Netherlands in October 1944 many of the NSB knew that the defeat of their German allies was inevitable and that retribution as traitors awaited them.

Arthur Seyss-Inquart was an Austrian Nazi who served as the civilian governor of the Netherlands and oversaw the brutal policies of the German occupiers. Jews were transported to concentration camps in Germany and Poland and the efficiency of the Germans and their Dutch collaborators meant that a higher proportion of Dutch Jews died than in any other Western European country. Concentration camps were established at Vught and Amersfoort. A general strike in February 1941 protesting attacks on the Jewish population in Amsterdam was ruthlessly suppressed and the organizers shot. Resistance actions such as the assassination of prominent collaborators or attacks on the occupying forces were met with reprisal executions specifically authorized by Seyss-Inquart. He was subsequently tried at Nuremberg, found guilty of war crimes and executed.

I slept that night in the hayloft and the following morning the effects of many cups of milk combined with many lovely apples made themselves manifest and, after a lot of awkwardness trying to explain that I needed to use a toilet without knowing the Dutch words for it, I was initiated to the Dutch watercloset – a fine institution. In fact they even risked taking me into the house for meals clad in a pair of overalls – my clothes were drying in the oven. The remainder of the time was spent in talking to the English-speaking boy and learning the lie of the land with regard to the Germans – and sleeping.

The prevailing situation was that 13 hostages had been seized in the neighbourhood the morning I had been found, and a proclamation issued saying that 600 workers were required within the next 48 hours to dig fortifications at Zevenaar – between Arnhem and Wesel. To assist people in making up their minds, bands of NSB supported by German parachutists were out 'visiting', which entailed marching into a house and removing all males between sixteen and sixty years of age at gunpoint.

This brought home to me how dangerous it was to stay where I was. That night the problem was solved by the arrival of two men, one of them dapper and well dressed[11] who asked for my name and number, the other a veritable Hercules (whose name I never discovered). Having shown them my credentials – an identity card and my faithfully preserved ripcord – I was once again handed my clothes, which were then donned.

140

Next, I was led outside and sat in the carrier of a large tradesman's bicycle, Hercules climbed into the saddle, and off we went into the darkness. There then ensued a most nightmarish bike ride down narrow rutted lanes, through little paths in wooded country, over narrow bridges – always in the knowledge that I would take the first impact if we hit anything. Hercules was unperturbed and pressed on, his country-trained eyes seeing where mine saw not, and his front wheel feeling for the path and making a light unnecessary. We couldn't use one anyway as we needed to remain un-detected.

At length I was led from the bike to the side of another strange barn. A beehive was lifted from its place, the ledge upon which it stood was raised, and a yawning hole revealed. Hercules motioned for me to enter. It was a dark vault 12 feet long and 3 feet high – an underground bread oven from long ago. Hercules showed me the air holes and relief bottles, bedding, and brought me porridge, then shut the lid and replaced the bee-hive. I was 'Underground'.

Chapter 13

Joining the Resistance

In the morning the farmer's wife removed the beehive from the trapdoor to give me some bread and water. I was sitting up in the bread oven below the trapdoor and this was the first time that she had seen me. I was in a rough physical state, with a split lip, cuts and bruises – not a pretty sight. In a very natural way she put her hand on my head in a comforting, maternal way. I burst into tears. I had been shot down, accepted that my close friend Ron was probably dead, and coped with the experience of being on the run through Germany, without allowing myself to feel any pity for my own situation, and this simple gesture of affection unlocked the self-control that I'd imposed on myself.

I remained in the bread oven a second day and night, until on the third night the beehive was again removed by the farmer and I was introduced to a man who, by signs and limited speech, indicated that I was to be taken elsewhere. We set off on foot and walked for about an hour to another hamlet called Lintelo, where we arrived at yet another farm.

There by the light of an oil lamp on the kitchen table I was introduced to the farmer Hendrick Diepenbroek, his wife Gerda, and two other men, Jan Ket and Ben te Brinke. Jan was a short, stocky, dark chap (his nickname was Swart Jan or Black John because of the colour of his hair) with a very animated forceful manner.

Ben was a farm labourer, tall, strong and muscular. Like Jan, Ben dressed as a farm worker and one could picture him on a farm slowly dealing with the challenges of the day in a lethargic manner, possibly chewing a straw as he did so – but nothing could be further from the truth. He had a brain that could move like lightning, as I was later to discover.

Jan seemed to be in charge. He asked for my name and I replied 'Humphrey', the name by which I was known in my family.

This seemed to trouble him and he asked: 'Have you another name, Humphrey is not a Dutch or German name?'

To this I replied, 'Francis.'

He thought for a moment and said, 'Here we will call you Frank.'

The reason for this renaming was simple. If Jan wanted to call across the street to me in the nearby town of Aalten, for instance, with Dutch people mingling with German soldiers and perhaps even the odd policeman, he could hardly shout the name 'Humphrey' without attracting attention. So Frank I became during my time in Holland and have remained in much of my business life since.

After this initial discussion I was taken up through a trapdoor, to a hiding place 12 feet by 12 feet in a boarded-up corner of the roof of the farmhouse. There was a rope across the space, with a blanket over the rope forming a curtain dividing the space in two. I was told to stay quiet because there was someone on the other side of the blanket. I slept through the night; at daylight the next day the blanket was pulled aside and I found that there was a sixteen-year-old Jewish girl whose parents had both been arrested. She was hiding in the farmhouse, helping the farmer's wife during the day by looking after the children and doing housework, and was able to stay there until the end of the war when she went to live in Israel.

The next day while sitting in the kitchen, Jan beckoned me to follow him out and together we went up the steps to the hiding place in the roof. There we sat facing each other on the thin layer of straw that passed for a bed at night for Jan, Ben and myself. Jan had a pleasant face and a ready smile and it was his aura of confidence and competence that struck one immediately. When he gave an order it may have been given in a quiet voice, and perhaps with a little quip of humour, but the look in his eyes made it quite clear that it had to be done, while his powerful hands suggested that he himself was ready for any task. After the war I met Douglas Bader and Jan had the same sort of personal charisma and no-nonsense attitude as Bader (although Jan was perhaps smarter and less egotistical). While wearing the same sort of clothes as the farming people in that part of Holland, Jan always wore a Breton-style sailor's cap and he was invariably to be seen with a cigarette in his mouth, rolled himself. These were his trademarks.

Happily Jan spoke English, or his special form of English. He had a good command of nouns but his vocabulary suffered from a shortage of verbs, so when in doubt he used his own special verb, which was 'I don't'. So if I asked him, for example 'How will we go to Aalten?', he might reply 'I don't a car', or if I asked 'What are you going to do tonight?', he would reply 'I don't some cigarettes for the boys.' We got along fine.

Jan looked at me with great intensity and in his limited, but quite understandable, English, began to question me. 'What are the names of the British and American bombers?'

I realised at once why he was doing this as we had been briefed that the Germans sometimes tried to interpose people masquerading as English into escape lines and resistance groups and Jan was trying to confirm that I was who I said I was. All aircrew had lectures on how to behave in this type of situation. I subsequently found out that just as I had received briefings on what to do in this sort of situation, the Resistance themselves had received training through the Special Operations Executive (SOE) on what sort of questions they should ask to confirm the genuineness of purported escapers.

I reeled off the names: 'Lancaster, Halifax, Flying Fortress, Liberator and Mosquito.'

'And what about Jagers [fighters]?' he asked.

I added, 'Hurricanes, Spitfires, Mustangs and Thunderbolts.'

And what did I know about infantry weapons, would I name and describe them? I replied that I had used Lee Enfield and Browning rifles, Bren guns, Browning automatic rifles and Webley .38 pistols. Then I ran into trouble.

He handed me a pencil and paper; 'Draw me a Tommy gun.' I thought that he wanted me to draw the Thompson sub-machine gun favoured by Al Capone and other Chicago gangsters in the days of Prohibition. I started to draw such a weapon and it was evident that my response troubled Jan. A sudden hardness came into his voice and he questioned me further. There was no doubt in my mind that he too was familiar with the weapons that he was asking me about. It then dawned on me that he was expecting me to draw a Sten gun, the cheap, simple mass-produced gun that the English paratroopers – 'Tommies' – used and which the SOE supplied to resistance movements all over Europe. The Sten guns fired bullets quickly, but at a low velocity and were notoriously unreliable. I was later told by a friend who had been involved in the Mau Mau Uprising in Kenya in the 1950s that the Mau Mau discovered that two stolen British Army greatcoats were sufficient to make a suit of 'armour' that would keep out the low-velocity bullets fired from a Sten gun – but you got a nasty bruise!

As soon as I understood what Jan was looking for, I drew a Sten gun, which seemed to satisfy him.

And so the questioning went on for perhaps half an hour. A silence then ensued while he continued to stare hard at me before he eventually brought my interrogation to an end.

Jan then left the Diepenbroek farmhouse and was away for several days, while I continued to stay in the attic hiding place at night. The Diepenbroeks had another concealed space behind the

146

boards of a pen for goats in a farm outbuilding close to the house. I can still recall the all-pervading smell of goats, which would have put off any searcher (later we used this hiding place to store weapons). The farm, like the other Dutch farms I was to stay on, was swarming with flies from the livestock and there were flypapers everywhere. It was a very different world from what I was used to.

During the day I helped the Diepenbroeks with jobs like chopping wood in the farmyard. They were small farmers (literally) with two small children. They were very friendly, but spoke no English, and at this stage I spoke no Dutch.

Jan may have checked my identity with London as I believe that his resistance unit had access to a radio operator who could pass messages to the capital. My family never received any indication from the authorities that I was still alive. The practice was that even if MI9 found out that an escaped airman was still alive they would not inform his family as they were afraid of the Germans somehow finding out that he was on the run. I was dreadfully concerned at what my family were going through. When our aircraft did not return my parents were sent a standard letter informing them that I was missing. My mother was confident that I was still alive and would be able to get back home; my father, with his experience of the realities of the First World War, was more pessimistic about my chances of survival.

On his return Jan now seemed satisfied with my bona fides and commenced a second, less tense, interview.

He asked did I know Morse code? When I nodded he quickly said, 'What is the code for Z?' To which I replied: 'Da Da Dot Dot.' He smiled and our discussion became more relaxed, Jan explaining that he was the leader of an active resistance group and that they would value my help if I was prepared to throw in my lot with them. They were expecting a parachute drop of arms and equipment but they needed a signaller who knew Morse code, could operate a lamp and spoke English.

He said that I must understand that it was a hard business and the chances of survival were poor. If I joined the Resistance I must bear in mind that I would not be covered by the Geneva Convention if I was captured carrying a gun and wearing civilian clothes. Before being shot I would be tortured by the Germans so they could extract information from me and find out who had hidden me. They would want to get information out of me within the first three days after being captured, before the Resistance realised that I had been caught and could make arrangements for the people I knew to go into hiding.

Jan would say, 'Give no names and ask no questions, you can't give away what you don't know.' I assured him that I would say nothing, to which he replied, 'You do not know these devils.' This sounded like melodramatic Hollywood stuff to me at the time, but of course Jan knew what he was talking about. Many resistance groups in Occupied Europe were discovered by the Gestapo and in the Netherlands the Germans had compromised major networks established by the

SOE earlier in the war, with many British and Dutch agents being sent to their deaths. Jan's achievement in running a network with no German penetration was almost unique.

In the Netherlands, German military intelligence, the Abwehr, compromised major networks run by the SOE in an operation known as *Das Englandspeil* (The England Game), also called *Unternehmen Nordpol* (Operation North Pole). Throughout the war Dutch agents who had been trained by the SOE in the United Kingdom were parachuted into the Netherlands, or in some case dropped ashore by motorboat. In 1942 the Germans captured an agent, Hebert Lauwers, and sent false transmissions back to SOE headquarters in the agent's name. Tragically the SOE failed to notice that these did not include standard security checks – a code word or phrase that confirmed the genuineness of the transmission. The absence of the check should have indicated to the SOE that the sender of the transmission had been compromised but SOE headquarters ignored the warning. SOE continued to transport Dutch agents in reliance on the false transmissions from the Abwehr and more than fifty agents were immediately arrested and in most cases executed. A high number of the RAF aircraft dropping them were also shot down. It was not until 1943 that two captured agents were able to escape from the concentration camp where they had been held and make their way back to the United Kingdom. Belatedly the SOE realized that something was amiss and ceased to rely on the compromised (and non-existent) network of agents. The climate of distrust resulting from this operation may have led the British to distrust intelligence from the Dutch Resistance prior to the battle of Arnhem.

I was a law-abiding young man and tended to do things by the book. I tried to remember what rules applied to such a situation. I could recall something of the relevant sections of the Air Force Act. These were periodically read to all personnel, usually in my experience by a fierce warrant officer who with great relish laid emphasis on the misdemeanours, such as desertion in the face of the enemy 'for which the penalty is death'. From what I could recall, the legislation said that if behind enemy lines, one's duty was to make every attempt to return to friendly territory and make oneself available to whatever unit was encountered. There was no specific guidance as to the exact situation I found myself in, with partisans in Occupied territory, but I judged that the correct thing to do would be to join Jan's group. With my knowledge of Morse code and aircraft I knew that I could be useful in helping to arrange drops of arms to them. So I agreed to join. I didn't hesitate at all in saying 'Yes' to Jan's request.

Jan then gave me a Mauser 32-mm pistol, with the advice that I should only use it to save myself from capture and, that if capture was inevitable, I should always keep one last bullet in the chamber to use on myself. I thought that Jan's stories of torture and using one's pistol on oneself if apprehended were straight out of a gangster movie. Even though I was repeatedly warned, I didn't

150

really grasp at the time how ruthless the Germans really were. We had lectures and films on the squadron showing how the enemy would interrogate prisoners and warning that we should not give away anything more than rank and serial number. Unfortunately, the films were so corny that they were difficult to take seriously – after the war I heard stories of RAF prisoners bursting into laughter when the real Germans asked the same questions as their counterparts in the training films. I'm not sure that the Germans appreciated the humour of this.

Notwithstanding Jan's advice not to ask unnecessary questions, later I found out more about him and the resistance unit that he commanded. Jan had joined the Dutch Navy before the war as a seaman and through his natural gift of leadership had progressed to the rank of Warrant Officer by the time the Germans invaded Holland in 1940. He was a submariner and his submarine was in dock when a force of German airborne troops attacked the dockyard. Jan rounded up as many of his crew as he could and engaged the Germans. He was wounded and taken to hospital, subsequently becoming a prisoner when the Germans captured the port. On his release at the end of 1940 he obtained employment in the Customs Service and worked in the Dutch/German customs control stations in the vicinity of Aalten, where he was ideally placed to help Allied aircrew escape and to play his part in the activities of the Resistance, which he did with notable success. Jan's group had been active in the Battle of Arnhem, removing a section of railway line to wreck a train bringing supplies to the Germans, so they were wanted men.

When I met him he'd already had some narrow escapes. Once he was going by car with three other partisans to Hertogenbosch to meet with the White Brigade, another underground group who were taking Jews and aircrew to Brussels. His car was stopped and he and Ben te Brinke were loaded into a German truck with two soldiers positioned on the tailgate. Jan was handcuffed but found that he could push his hands down between the body of the truck and its canvas roof and unhitch a length of canvas. When the truck stopped Jan and Ben stood up and jumped backwards through the gap Jan had created between the canvas roof and side of the truck. Jan and Ben got away in different directions but the other two partisans in the truck did not escape and were executed by the Germans at the prison at Vught, part of a concentration camp. I visited Vught prison after the war and found it a very sinister place with poles in a yard that prisoners were chained to before being shot. No doubt I would have ended up at Vught prison, or a place like it, if I had ever been caught myself by the Germans.

There was a story behind the Mauser pistol that Jan gave me. Jan and Ben had been surrounded in a house by the Germans and burst out through the door firing their pistols as they escaped. Jan hit one of the Germans in the mouth with a bullet from his Mauser, but as he said to me, 'German didn't die', which left him greatly dissatisfied with the gun's performance. After giving me the Mauser he got a heavy-calibre Colt 45 from our stock of weapons for his own use, no doubt hoping that it would pack a heavier punch than the Mauser.

Why were these resistance members running huge risks at a relatively late stage in the war when it was obvious to everyone that the Allied forces would soon be crossing the Rhine and bringing the war to an end? They were dedicated men, very loyal to Holland, and motivated by a great hatred of the Germans. I think that they wanted to remedy some of the humiliation that the Dutch had suffered through more than four years of occupation. They considered it right to form into small military groups that could take an active role in securing the liberation of their country. Their intention was that when the combat got close they could be useful in fighting immediately behind the German front lines.

Chapter 14

Resistance Work

As I had hoped, I was able to help Jan's group with the arms deliveries that they were getting. A few days after my arrival word came that a parachute drop was expected. We listened to the midday BBC news and heard coded messages like 'Mary had a little lamb' or 'Father Christmas comes but once a year' read out. People in England would hear these strange communications on BBC broadcasts and wonder what on earth it all meant. In our case we listened for the message 'What has Peter's brother brought', which told us to expect a parachute drop of arms and ammunition at our predetermined dropping zone. The midday news message would be reconfirmed after the 6 p.m. news, together with another phrase indicating the period of the night that the drop would be made. The secret radio we used was in fact a car radio using a car battery, and keeping this charged was far from easy.

Parachute drops were on moonlit nights so we could see a little in the dark despite the blackout. At 10 p.m. a group of about fifteen men arrived at the farm where we were hiding and together with a horse and cart we set off along lanes and farm tracks to the dropping zone about an hour's walk away. The cart had motor vehicle rubber tyres and the horse's hooves were wrapped in sacking tied to its fetlocks with string to reduce noise. It was a cold, still night and the moon meant that we could see quite well. The curfew had started at 9 p.m. and we sent a couple of scouts ahead to ensure that we did not run into any Germans or NSB police. All of us, including me, were armed, and of course rather excited by the venture. I felt conscious of the need to maintain the British reputation of 'sangfroid' and did my best to give the impression that this was nothing more than a routine night's work for me.

Finding a suitable dropping zone in a heavily populated country like the Netherlands was challenging. The site was chosen to be well away from habitation, as German troops were billeted

154

everywhere. Even so there was a German radar tower close by, and I was told that the Germans used the field as a rifle range.

My role was to help the group lay out a flare path using men with torches in a line pointing into the wind, each man about 100 metres from the next, with myself 100 metres to the left of the head of the line with a signalling torch. The torches were in long, narrow wooden boxes, roughly 50 centimetres long, 10 centimetres wide and 10 centimetres deep. We had fitted a torch in each box so that the handle of the torch stuck out from the base. At the bottom and the top ends of the box there were nails, each protruding out a couple of centimetres, which could be used like a gun sight to line up the torch. As the aircraft arrived each man would aim his torch box at the aircraft as it circled the dropping zone, the box meant that the beam of light from the torch could not be seen on either side. So any German observer could be relatively close to the field and still not see the origins of the lights because they were being pointed directly at the circling aircraft. I understand that the layout of the flare paths was standard in resistance groups through-out Europe and this ingenious technique had been taught by the SOE to someone in Jan's group. I now realise that our group was on the outer fringes of SOE's operations in Europe.

The plan was that I would flash the required Morse code message from the ground to signal the aircraft to confirm our dropping zone. Having established contact with the aircraft, on my command all torches would be aimed at the

155

aircraft as it made a wide circuit to line up with the flight-path for the drop.

I was very keyed up but didn't feel frightened, as the whole operation seemed to be carefully managed in a most military fashion. There were sentries placed around the drop zone on the alert for any sign of Germans and Jan had the group very well disciplined.

Several times I thought I could hear an aircraft approaching but it was just my imagination. Finally, at about 1 a.m. I heard the characteristic (and relatively quiet) sound of Bristol Hercules engines approaching and a Short Stirling bomber emerged out of the darkness, flying at about 500 feet. The Stirling aircraft was used because of the capacious bomb bays and they performed best at low level. I started flashing out a signal in Morse code and called for the men to form the flare path. It worked exactly as planned. The aircraft made its circuit, then with bomb doors open, still very low, it lined up with the flare path and commenced its dropping run. I could see the rear gunner in his turret as it passed over. I felt a wave of emotion and a lump in my throat at the thought that I was just a few hundred feet from fellow RAF flyers, who would be returning home to England in a matter of hours and sitting down to a fry-up for breakfast with cups of tea and 'Jane' in the *Mirror*.

As the containers came out of the aircraft their parachutes opened to slow their descent, but two or three of the twenty-nine containers burst open while still in the air with the shock of the parachute canopies abruptly opening and arresting

156

their fall. The men lined up along the flare path were showered with Sten guns, rifles, boxes of ammunition and even food like corned beef and chocolates packed in tins, as the contents of the broken containers were flung far and wide. Most fortunately, no one was injured. We first rolled up the parachutes and piled them on the cart, then we picked up the containers, which took four men to carry. Then forming up a line a few paces apart we slowly, and methodically, walked across the field picking up everything that had burst from the splintered containers. There were guns sticking barrel first into the ground, which we pulled out just like cabbages. Given the Germans' use of the field as a rifle range we had to make certain that everything was retrieved, that all the containers and their parachutes were accounted for, and no traces of our presence were left after the parachute drop was completed. We loaded everything on the cart, and then on the way home – following side roads and staying off any main highways – we hid half the contents from the containers under a haystack at a farm and the remainder in a hideaway in a pigsty at another smallholding.

From records I found after the war I believe that the date of this drop was the night of 25/26 October 1944 and the Stirling aircraft was from 190 Squadron of 38 Group, a specialist Airborne Support Unit with a crew from the Royal Canadian Air Force.

In early November, through coded messages sent after BBC news reports, we learnt that another supply drop was to take place on the same drop zone. Again there were about fifteen men gathered at the site and we were all armed. The pattern followed that of the previous delivery. It was a Short Stirling bomber and, again, several of the containers burst open above our heads, showering their contents on our party. This time, however, the aircraft was late and by the time the cart was loaded and we set off home it was starting to get light. Hiding our guns we found ourselves sauntering along the country roads on a fine, crisp autumnal morning in the company of people going to Sunday morning church. I felt very vulnerable walking around in broad daylight with our conspicuous cargo and wearing my navy blue overalls among the church folk in their formal dark suits and hats. I can only assume that they knew what we were up to as no one in that close-knit community betrayed us.

After the second supply drop I returned to the farm with soaking-wet shoes. The parlour stove had gone out, but was still warm, so I put my shoes on the top to dry. Unfortunately, when I went to put the shoes on the next day I found the soles had cracked. This may sound trivial but Jan was furious with my carelessness as shoes were a precious commodity in Occupied Holland. The shoes had to be taken to a cobbler to be resoled. As there were no nails available, this had to be done using hundreds of thorns. For most of the rest of my time in Holland I wore wooden clogs like the other farm workers.

Altogether there were three supply drops while I was there and we received enough guns and ammunition to arm about seventy men. On a couple of occasions we picked up messages that an air drop was coming and prepared for the delivery, but the aircraft did not appear – it was a pretty hazardous game for the airmen supplying us. I'm not sure if the plane's absence was because it had been shot down or if there were other reasons for the non-appearance. Later in the RAF I heard about one incident when an aircraft on a drop for the SOE was flying so low that it almost hit the dyke across the Zuider Zee. Standing waiting almost all night for the arrival of the aircraft in the dark, cold and wet, and then having to go home empty-handed was not the happiest of experiences for us on the ground, and I was very conscious of the risks that the airmen were also running.

I was in G.H. Diepenbroek's farmhouse for some weeks, spending most of the daytime out and about unless the situation was particularly dangerous. One day I was in the farmyard chopping up firewood when a P51 Mustang flew low overhead, leaving a trail of smoke. The plane turned upside down and I saw the pilot bail out and his parachute open. Jan and Ben were with me and indicated that I should stay in the farmhouse while they would try to get the pilot before the Germans could find him. Ominously I could hear the engines of German vehicles in the area starting up as they went to look for the pilot. Men were shouting and blowing whistles and it was obvious that the search had begun.

I waited anxiously at the farmhouse, frustrated that I could not be out looking for my fellow airman. Half an hour later I saw Jan and Ben coming back without the pilot and I left the farmyard confines to meet them halfway down a farm track before we all turned back to walk towards the farm again. I was level with a haystack when suddenly I saw two German soldiers on bicycles turn on to the track. Quick as a flash Ben pushed me off the pathway behind the haystack, while the Germans dismounted from their bicycles and came towards the Dutchmen to check their identification papers.

I was torn between trying to conceal myself and wanting to shoot the Germans before they found me. I hid behind the haystack and took my Mauser pistol out. Reasoning that the German soldiers were probably right-handed, I decided that my best plan was to watch for them coming from an anti-clockwise direction. I released the safety catch on my Mauser and was ready to pull the trigger, but held back as I knew that shooting was a last resort because of the risk that the Germans would carry out reprisals on everyone in the area if any of their soldiers were killed. My heart was pounding away, going nineteen to the dozen. I endeavoured to remain undetected by keeping the haystack between myself and the enemy. The soldiers checked Jan and Ben's papers, got back on their bikes, and cycled away. I was able to breathe again.

This was a bad moment but was all done so quickly that the Germans did not notice that the three Dutchmen in front of them had suddenly become only two. We were just 20 yards apart and I had seen them quite clearly before I was elbowed aside by Ben. Presumably they simply noticed a group of farm workers in front of them and it did not register that the number had changed.

That evening Jan rounded up four or five of our men and decided to look again for the pilot, who we guessed was hiding out in the woods. The Dutch didn't speak any English so I taught them to call out 'Come out you bugger we are your friends', which I thought that the American pilot would regard as a reassuring phrase that the Germans were unlikely to have come up with. This search was also unsuccessful but two days later a farmer from two miles away brought in the American pilot, Joe Davis. Joe had dislocated his knee in exiting from his aircraft and had hidden out in the woods as we suspected. He later told us that the Germans were very clever and they'd tried to get him to come out of hiding by calling out 'Come out you bugger we are your friends', but he had not been taken in by their tricks!

Joe was a gung-ho sort of character, full of bravado, which he never quite carried off successfully. Once, he got his hands on an enormous revolver, bigger even than Jan's Colt 45, and demonstrated to a group of our boys a cowboy twirl with the revolver, as in a Western movie. In executing this trick the gun went off accidentally and Joe was fortunate that the bullet passed between two men without hitting anyone. On another occasion, when we went to collect weapons from an arms drop, Joe insisted on demonstrating his military prowess by carrying a heavy Bren gun despite having a weak knee that had not yet mended. He ended up being ignominiously carried back to our home on a farm cart.

Joe was from the American South and the rest of us found his views on 'niggers' hard to take. For example, he told a grim story about going out on a lynching party with the Ku Klux Klan. It eventually came out that both his parents were blind and he had been brought up by a black nanny. Extraordinary! I suspect that some of Joe's bravado and other aspects of his character may have been motivated by insecurities from his background. Joe and I got on well enough at first when there were only the two of us, but later when there were seven airmen cooped up in a small space I frequently had to bite my tongue because he was so noisy and opinionated. Joe was the most experienced pilot among us, as he made clear in conversation. The other Americans referred to him as 'the Big Wheel'. He seemed rather resentful when the Dutch tended to turn to me instead of himself as the principal representative of the group of fliers. He was undoubtedly tough, and subsequent events showed how self-possessed he could be in a crisis. Had our situation ever resulted in a shoot-out with the enemy, there is no doubt that he would have fought courageously and well, and this is perhaps the acid test.

Chapter 15

The Prinzens

After Joe's arrival we realised that the Germans would be searching the neighbourhood, continuing to look for him, so Jan arranged for us both to be taken to a farm called Samsonhuis where Bernard and Dora Prinzen lived with their children. We arrived at Samsonhuis in the early hours of the morning and, so as not to disturb the family, we were led to a barn containing farm machinery that had an empty room in the hayloft (we later moved to a different building, immediately adjacent to the farmhouse, and it was this building that became our hiding place for the next few months). We lay down on the floor and dozed for a few hours. I was awakened by noises below and went to the window. My very first sight of Bernard Prinzen was of a middle-aged man wearing his Sunday best black suit, complete with a top hat, harnessing the farm horse to an ancient carriage – it looked like a scene from the nineteenth century. He set off shortly afterwards and we later learnt that he used this conveyance to carry the principal mourners behind the hearse at a funeral. Today this task might be performed by a Rolls-Royce or Mercedes. No doubt it was a nice little earner for Bernard.

Soon children started appearing, and we went

down to meet the family and have breakfast in their warm kitchen. And what a lovely family they proved to be. Bernard and Dora were in their forties and they had ten children ranging in age from their attractive daughter, Truida, who was twenty, to the youngest, Benny, who was about six. There were four girls: Truida, Hermein, Johanna and Anna, and six boys – Hendrick, Jan, Derk, Willum, Marinus and Benny.

We lived in the hiding place in their barn with a Dutchman named Albert who, like the two eldest Prinzen boys, had not registered as a worker in the Arbeitsdienst compulsory labour scheme.

The Prinzens and other farmers who took us in were part of a very religious community with strong loyalty to their country and Queen. They regarded the Germans as the force of evil; they used to ask 'What business have they got to be in our country?' In their farmhouses, on a mantelpiece or dresser in the kitchen, there would be an empty biscuit tin with a portrait of Queen Wilhelmina. This was a very political statement at a time when the Queen and royal family were in exile in London. They admired Churchill for standing up to the Germans and looked to England for their liberation. By hiding me and other airmen they felt they could contribute to aiding England without firing a gun.

I warmed to the Dutch stoic opposition to the Germans at every turn, their generosity of spirit and, of course, their courage in looking after aircrew and the airborne troops after Arnhem. We seemed to be similar to the Dutch culturally and shared a liking for football. In contrast my

164

attitude towards the Germans, never positive, hardened further. The Dutch drew some distinction between the ordinary German Army, and the SS and Gestapo, but generally felt a bitter hatred towards what the Germans had done in their country. I shared this feeling and we all assumed that at the end of the war the SS and Gestapo would be held accountable for their crimes and that many would be executed.

The landscape around the Prinzen farm was not completely flat, like most of the rest of the Netherlands; there were slight undulations, with open farmland interspersed with woodlands towards the east in the direction of Germany. I was there over a number of months in autumn, winter and early spring so my memories are of a bare, austere landscape dominated by the big sky overhead. The vast majority of the farms in the district were relatively small, with farmhouses and barns often linked together in a 'T' shape. The cattle in the barn over the winter months generated heat that warmed the humans in the adjacent farmhouse. There were no grand houses in the neighbourhood apart from a house near Aalten that General Model used as his headquarters.

The Prinzen farm was typical for the area, about 15 acres in size. As well as the farm horse we had seen Bernard hitching up to the funeral carriage, they had about 15 pigs, 10 cows, and numerous chickens. They grew everything they could to support themselves, even tobacco, which they tried to dry in the barn (not very successfully as it tended to get mildew in the damp) and use to make cigars. Even without the added strains of the harsh wartime conditions, the Prinzens, and their neighbours, lived a very modest and frugal existence.

It was easy to see that the Netherlands was in a desperate situation in late 1944 and early 1945 – the period of the 'Hongerwinter' (Hunger Winter). The northern part of the country remained under German occupation while the southern half was mostly liberated. The front line went as far as the Rhine after the failed Market Garden operation, with the British and Canadians on the south side of the river and the Germans on the other. Samsonhuis was near a small town called Dinxperlo to the south-east of Aalten, and so close to the German border that with local knowledge one could cross the frontier at night in twenty minutes or so. I was in no hurry to return to Germany, and had no occasion to do so, but if the Prinzen boys had advance warning of an impeding 'razzier' (search) of our area they would slip across the border to stay with an aunt who had married a German farmer and lived on the German side.

At this stage of the war the British Second Army, having failed to break through and reach the 1st Airborne Division at Arnhem, held the bridge across the Maas River at Nijmegen and had reached the west bank of the Rhine. Where we were hidden was only fifteen miles or so from the front line so there were always large numbers of German soldiers in the vicinity.

The Germans were using forced labour to fortify the most obvious Rhine crossing points

166

where there were (or had been) bridges, and laying minefields in between. Dutchmen were being rounded up by the Germans and NSB and told to make their way to camps where the work was taking place. Zevenaar was one such labour camp and we heard that the forced labourers were housed in primitive conditions and badly fed.

To put a stop to this process Jan's resistance unit established road blocks at night where these workers were turned back at gunpoint with instructions to tell the Nazis that this was under the orders of the Dutch Army of Liberation. Most of the workers arrived on bicycles and, if they protested too vehemently at being turned back, their bicycles would be confiscated by the resistance unit. I became aware of this activity as Joe and I were made responsible for taking care of the confiscated bicycles and hiding them in a barn.

In the meantime, the Nazi Governor of the Netherlands, Arthur Seyss-Inquart was bleeding the country white by shipping foodstuffs to Germany, leaving the major cities to starve. It was difficult to distribute the remaining food because of the dislocation of the railway system as a result of railway workers going on strike, and the Allied air attacks. This led to the spectacle of young people walking long distances from the cities to our part of the country with haversacks on their backs, hoping to buy or acquire a few kilos of potatoes and a slice of spek (salted pork) to take back to Amsterdam or wherever they lived. Such people frequently called at Samson-huis and were an added worry because of the risk

167

that their visit would lead to discovery of the hiding airmen. They stood out as being genuine by the way they walked – I soon noticed that starving people walk bent forwards. The deaths of approximately 18,000 people in Occupied Holland over this period were attributed primarily to the effects of malnutrition.

We were better off at Samsonhuis but food was still scarce, and feeding escaped airmen who were not entitled to official rations must have been an additional challenge for the Prinzens. We normally had two slices of bread for breakfast with butter made on the farm. Mother Prinzen would bring out a jar of apple mousse and we could put a scraping of this or perhaps a thin slice of cheese or spek on our bread. Lunch was usually boiled potatoes with some slices of carrot, over which would be poured gravy from melted pork fat. A sausage for lunch was a major treat. Supper would be another two slices of bread, while before bed, as often as not, we would be given a bowl of what in Scotland would be called gruel – thin porridge made with oats and milk, called 'pap' by us. Interestingly, when I returned to visit the Prinzens after the war I found that the food I was offered was much the same as during wartime.

Cups of coffee appeared during the day, taking the form of ersatz (substitute) coffee bought from the shops, or homemade from roasted acorns. Neither actually tasted of coffee and we tried to recall what real coffee tasted like. There was invariably a coffee pot on the go on the hot kitchen stove, stoked with the wood that we chopped on a daily basis.

We never went truly hungry, but food was an ever-present topic of conversation among us and we dreamt of steaks and bacon and eggs. It was a particular shock to me, as in the RAF we were not subject to rationing and were well fed, eating bacon and eggs for breakfast every day. I recall a lunch later during our stay, when a new airman, Owen Mayberry, had just arrived, and we were given two slices of bread. Owen innocently buttered his bread, added multiple slices of cheese and ham, and then spread on a generous helping of apple mousse. Everyone else looked on in amazement as he built up an enormous American-style club sandwich. Afterwards we had to explain to him that one had either a slice of cheese, or one of ham, or a thinly spread helping of apple mousse – but not all of them at once. At the Prinzens' farm we ate what the family ate and I trust that we showed our gratitude for their generosity and selflessness.

We settled into a daily routine of farm life, helping out by milking cows (something I had never done before and didn't demonstrate any natural talent for), taking turns in churning milk to make butter, cleaning out stalls, chopping wood, peeling a bucket of potatoes every day for the ten adults and ten children staying at the farm, and doing other chores around the property. We seldom strayed beyond the farmyard during the day as we did not want to put the Prinzens at risk with the sort of random encounter I had had at the Diepenbroeks' farm. We spent much of our time in the hiding place in the barn cleaning the guns that had been dropped to Jan's resistance group. There was always an arsenal of Sten guns, Bren guns and even a bazooka kept there, along with hundreds of rounds of ammunition. We stored further guns and ammunition in a hole in the ground concealed underneath one of the haystacks in the farm.

The Prinzens' farm became a focal point to which escaping airmen were directed, and another American P51 pilot, Bobby Brown, joined us there soon afterwards. Like Joe Davis, Bobby had hurt his knee when he parachuted from his aircraft. Both pilots left their P51s by turning the plane upside down but then got tangled up and hit the tailplane, injuring knees at that point rather than when they hit the ground on landing. Bobby had been captured by the Germans and put in the local hospital, where he wasn't very popular in a ward filled with German soldiers, many of whom had been wounded by Allied aircraft. To ensure that the Germans did not realise that his damaged knee had improved, Bobby insisted on the medical orderlies helping him to move around until he felt strong enough to try to escape. One night Bobby managed to slip out of bed, put on the uniform of an injured German soldier who was in an adjoining bed and had placed his uniform in a bedside locker, and then creep out the front door of the hospital. Wearing this German uniform, Bobby walked a quarter of a mile and then knocked at the door of a house at random and said that he was an American pilot on the run from the Germans. Greatly alarmed, the Dutch occupants of the house nevertheless hid him for two or three days and then, because his injured leg made it difficult for him to pedal, he was towed much of the way on a bicycle to our farmhouse.

Bobby was an amateur boxer who had competed in the famous Golden Gloves boxing tournaments in the United States. He was short and stocky with a slightly squashed nose from his pugilistic days. Bobby had a lively personality; he radiated vitality and good humour.

I recall a story that Bobby told us about his father who was unemployed during the Depression and had taken the opportunity to go to work in a remote logging camp in Washington State as part of one of Roosevelt's New Deal projects. His father was a big smoker but very hard up and not able to afford tobacco paper for the cigarettes that he made. Instead his wife had given him a Bible to take to the camp, and when he eventually returned to his family he told Bobby that he'd 'smoked his way through the Bible' as he'd used up every page on cigarettes. Apparently he never informed his wife of the fate of her gift; she wouldn't have been impressed had she known.

Bobby's dad had died so, now as the head of his family, he was worried about how his mother and 'kid sister' Lorraine, were faring in his absence – he always said that he 'didn't want anyone messing around with Lorraine (When he got back to the States after the war Bobby was relieved to find that one of his friends, Ray, who met with his approval, had married Lorraine.) If I ever got away without Bobby I was tasked with looking after the 'kid sister'. Bobby was a lovely, cheerful chap who I took to immediately and we got on very well – I've always admired the positive side of the American character. He used to tease me about the way I spoke, trying to impersonate my British public school accent by saying 'frightfully' and 'jolly good show' with a plum in his mouth. I did my best to retaliate with my rendition of a southern drawl based on my time in the South of the United States.

Chapter 16

Night-time Expeditions

The resistance unit led by Jan and his second in command, Long Henk, had taken over an unused, semi-derelict barn called De Berk, around ten minutes walk from Samsonhuis and they only ventured out from this hideout at night. As well as Dutchmen the group of about twenty-five included two Poles and two Frenchmen. Later, the group hiding there was joined by two men from Alsace-Lorraine who had deserted from the German Army, and two girls, who had been camp followers of the Germans but had decided to escape from them. One of the girls was pregnant and in March 1945, when we had to evacuate De Berk, the girls were hidden in a local convent until the end of the war.

Once or twice a week we went out at night to weapons training sessions at De Berk. I was able to show the Dutch how to use weapons that I was familiar with through my time in the Officer Training Corps at school and in the Home Guard. For instance, the Dutch had never seen Bren guns, but from my experience in handling the similar Browning machine guns I was able to instruct them in the use of the Brens that had been included in the SOE parachute drops. The weapons delivered to us included bazookas – the American equivalent of the British anti-tank weapon the PIAT (Projector, Infantry, Anti Tank) – which I hadn't had any previous experience with. The bazookas came with instruction books in English so I was able to figure out how they worked and teach the Dutch – they were a rocket weapon so went off with a 'woosh' rather than a bang. The Dutch got the hang of things pretty quickly, but I remember once there was an accident when someone accidentally pulled the trigger of a loaded Bren gun that had its safety catch off, and the burst of bullets put a 10-centimetre hole in the side of De Berk.

Jan also took us to other meetings that he arranged with local people at night before the curfew started at 9 p.m. This was a public relations exercise on his part. He needed to have the local population on his side in order to obtain money and food coupons to support the hidden airmen and resistance fighters. Looking after us was a significant burden in the conditions that existed over the winter of 1944/45. By showing us to people, Jan would be demonstrating the truth of his stories about sheltering Allied airmen. The British were very popular in the Netherlands; the fighting at Arnhem, although unsuccessful, had created a very favourable impression. Many Dutch civilians were inadvertently killed or injured in bombings, but there did not seem to be any resentment of aircrew. If a big formation of planes was going overhead people would come out and wave and the Dutch understood that bombing had been the main way for us to wage war against Germany in Europe before the D-Day landings.

One night I went with Jan into the local town, Aalten, and he stopped outside a house in a street of attached houses. Jan knocked on the door and we were admitted by a woman in her twenties and taken into a dining room where there was a long table, probably also used as a billiard table, with an elongated lampshade hanging over it. Jan and I sat down and the woman who let us in was joined by her sister and middle-aged mother. We were offered the usual acorn coffee and made polite conversation with the two daughters, who spoke some English, while the mother just smiled, beaming away at me. Then there was a knock at the front door and one of the daughters said, 'That's probably the lieutenant.' To my horror a German infantry officer, fair haired and in his early twenties, wearing a smart 'bum freezer' tunic, entered the room, courteously said good evening to everyone, and walked through the room on his way to the stairs leading up to what was apparently his bedroom. I was completely disconcerted by his arrival, but from the reaction of the other people around the table, I realised that his presence was entirely normal and that he didn't pose an immediate threat to us.

174

A few minutes later the German officer came back down the stairs and seated himself on the opposite side of the table from me. Jan and the girls continued speaking in Dutch for a few minutes, while I couldn't look the German in the face because the tassels of the lampshade obscured my view. I could only assume that he was a relatively innocuous German billeted with the family, but I was not totally at ease! This was the first time that I had been in the immediate proximity of an enemy soldier and I was comforted by the thought of my Mauser pistol tucked under my arm. The mother continued to smile away and seemed to be enjoying the situation. It was a surreal scene, but a tense experience for me at least and I did not easily recover from the initial shock of his appearance.

Finally Jan said to me (in Dutch, as by then I had acquired a bit of Dutch vocabulary), 'We should be heading off Frank.' Jan had a breton sailor's cap on and as he got to his feet he accidentally knocked this to the floor. When he bent over to pick up his cap I could see the butt of his Colt 45 sticking out of his jacket – I think it was obscured from the German's view, or he may have decided that it was better to exercise some discretion and ignore what he was seeing. We said goodbye to our hosts, went out the door, and then I started to breathe a bit more easily. I've often wondered how much the German lieutenant knew of what was going on – he certainly seemed more relaxed than I felt.

On another occasion Bobby Brown and I went to

a house with Jan where we had coffee with two middle-aged lady schoolteachers. We had acorn coffee and civil conversation. I could just about follow the dialogue, but like Jan I was not very adept at using verbs from a foreign language. When Jan had finished his business, we stepped out of the front door into the pitch-dark night and set off on our bikes in single file to get out of Aalten before the 9 p.m. curfew came into effect. As we pedalled down the street Bobby accidentally ran the front wheel of his bike on to some tramlines and fell off it. Jan and I went back to assist him, but in the meantime a number of people walking by on the pavement had gone to his aid, including a German soldier. I remember Bobby politely saying 'Danke schön' in a strong American accent to the helpful soldier as we hauled him away on his bike before his enthusiasm for conversation with the enemy gave us away.

One night Jan and I went into Aalten on our bikes and stopped in front of a substantial house opposite a school where Germans were billeted, and which had a German sentry outside. We went up a side alley to the back of the house and Jan tapped on a window. A woman opened it and Jan introduced me to his wife, Emmie. She was very lovely looking and the sight of her in the moonlight made a vivid impression on me. Jan was on the run, wanted by the police, and this was the only sort of fleeting contact that he was able to have with her. To support the family she ran the house as a care home for elderly ladies.

These expeditions were risky but good for our

spirit and I always came back from them feeling rejuvenated. In these outings there was something of the flavour of the adventures of Lawrence of Arabia, which had made such a great impression on me as a schoolboy, and I did enjoy them. I would have been keen to engage in acts of sabotage against the Germans but we knew that we had to hold back because of the risk of reprisals. Jan told me about a little town called Putten where the Resistance, helped by a British airborne sergeant from the Arnhem fighting, had ambushed a staff car carrying a Gestapo officer. In revenge the Germans rounded up more than 600 men and boys from the town and shipped them all off to concentration camps (from which less than 50 returned after the war).

Joe and another airman, Owen Mayberry, were present at Samsonhuis by this time but declined to come on the expeditions, no doubt because as married men they did not want to take what they considered to be unnecessary risks. I could understand Jan's purpose in undertaking them and I had confidence that he was not reckless and only introduced us to people whom he knew he could trust.

I was conscious that we were putting the Prinzen family in peril by staying with them. I was very worried that there were too many children about to be safe from the danger of one of the children inadvertently saying something to the wrong person and disclosing our presence – as in fact happened later. The children were not going to school, so there was no chance of them accidentally spilling the beans there, but some of the neighbours must have suspected that the Prinzens had Allied soldiers or airmen staying with them. There were placards displayed in local towns and villages saying that anyone helping escaped air-crew would be shot, so the family and our other friends were all running an enormous risk. I never suspected that anyone involved in Jan's resistance group would betray us. Jan was very rigorous in recruiting only people that he knew and trusted from within the close-knit local Protestant community. He was definitely prejudiced against outsiders and this meant that he didn't select many Jews (perhaps unfairly he thought that Jews were more likely to be doing deals to ensure their survival) or Catholics, although he can't have applied these rules too strictly as there were a number of Jews and Catholics in the group.

I discussed with Jan moving somewhere else where we would not be imperilling such a large family. He arranged for Joe and I to go to another farm run by Wilheim Hoftizer. He was a stocky, very busy and vital man; his wife Daatje was much taller and bigger and was very motherly towards us, as well as to her own children.

Wilheim was a local agricultural contractor with a business doing ploughing and similar work for farmers and hiring out equipment to them, with a side business repairing ploughs, tractors and other agricultural machinery. We used his work-shop behind the farmhouse to repair guns damaged in the supply drops. The hiding place at the Hoftizers' was over the pigsty, and the flies and smell of the pigs was not a great improvement on my experience of the goats at the Diepenbroeks'

178

farm. I cursed the Dutch for sensibly choosing hiding places that might be effective in discouraging close inspection by searchers, inevitably at the expense of the comfort of the sheltering airmen.

While I was staying at the Hoftizers' farm I got to know Jan's second in command, Hendrick van t'Lam, nicknamed Long Henk because he was so tall, and his friend Villem 'Mit de Brille' (with the spectacles). Long Henk had refused to register for labour with the authorities and found his way to eastern Holland where he established contact with Jan and his group. Henk was a big man with a corresponding large personality and strong character. He had a good command of English and lovely sense of humour, which he contrived to demonstrate with a fund of malapropisms such as claiming, 'I was as drunk as a door nail.'

After our first supply drop, Long Henk had been cycling to deliver a case of ammunition carried on the back of his bike to an outlying farm. On rounding a corner with banks on either side of the lane – preventing easy escape – he ran into a roadblock manned by four NSB policemen who demanded to see his identity papers. Being left-handed Long Henk reached into his right inside jacket pocket as though to pull out his papers but instead he drew out his Luger pistol and fired shots at each of the policemen, badly wounding three and scaring the fourth enough to make his escape. I never heard of any reprisals on the civilian population for this type of attack on the NSB policemen, as there would have been if

Germans had been involved.

Long Henk also led an expedition to burgle Aalten town hall. Late at night a small group of our men broke into the town hall where they stole blocks of identity cards and food coupons, which they marked with the official stamps before making their escape. These documents were important in enabling the hiding resistance men and fliers to be fed. By November 1944 Long Henk commanded the twenty-five or so resistance members quartered at the De Berk barn, which formed the central unit of the Aalten Resistance of around a hundred men. It was Long Henk's men who were on constant call should an emergency arise.

One day Joe and I were in the workshop at the Hoftizers' farm, working on a Bren gun that had been damaged in the supply drop, trying to bend the barrel in a vice to straighten it. We were absorbed in our work until I heard a disturbance outside and through a crack in the door I saw Wilheim grappling with four black-uniformed Dutch NSB police. They had arrived on their bikes so we hadn't any audible warning of their presence, but fortunately Wilheim had spotted the men and been able to intercept them before they came into the workshop. Wilheim, who was a little man, had the sergeant by the throat, and his rather more substantial wife Daatje joined in the struggle too, beating the NSB sergeant on the head with her fists. They were deliberately creating a lot of noise to alert us and give us time to get away. It was incredibly brave of the Hoftizers to fight with these armed men, knowing the likely consequences.

It would not have helped the situation for us to join Wilheim and Daatje; they were clearly creating a diversion to enable us to flee. I grabbed the gun from the vice, hid it under the bench, ran out of the back door with Joe, and we made good our escape across the fields. We could not run in our wooden shoes so had to take them off and hotfoot it in our socks. Returning to the farmhouse some hours later when we judged that the coast would be clear, we found Daatje in floods of tears. Wilheim had been arrested and taken to the local police station. From there he was sent to a labour camp for men who were employed building fortifications for the Germans on the north side of the Rhine.

Of course Daatje was greatly distressed and it was a traumatic experience for their children as well.

Chapter 17

Back to the Prinzens

Our narrow escape at the Hofitzers' occurred in December 1944 and meant that Joe and I needed to move back to the Prinzens' farm. Shortly before Christmas we were joined by Owen Mayberry and Ted Roblee, two American crewmen from a B17 Flying Fortress shot down near by. Owen was a B17 co-pilot and the biggest man among us. He had an easy, laid-back disposition and prior to joining the USAAF had been a technician in the aviation industry. He was very troubled knowing that his wife and baby daughter did not know whether he was alive or dead. This led him to decide not to participate in the occasional trips we made into Aalten at night or take part in parachute drops – he regarded these as unnecessary risks in his situation. Ted, the bombardier in the B17, was quiet and reserved but clearly highly intelligent. Coming from the same crew, Owen and Ted naturally were close.

St Nicholas's Eve on 5 December is the usual date for gift giving in the Netherlands, but the Prinzens made a big effort to celebrate Christmas with us on 24/25 December 1944 and make it a happy one for us all. The children decorated the house with greenery, and the aluminium Window strips from Allied bombers served as an admirable substitute for tinsel. Somehow the Prinzens were able to find special reserves of food and drink at a time of severe hardship. They gave me a pipe and tobacco as a gift, and a local clergyman, Dominie Klijn, visited us at the farm to take the Christmas-morning service. He read from the Gospel of Luke in both Dutch and English. Albert, the young Dutchman who was hiding with the family, played carols on a harmonium in the front parlour of the farmhouse, and the Resistance somehow managed to find some printed sheets of Christmas carol music with the words in English (Bobby was given these and kept them after the war). We sang carols like 'Hark the Herald Angels Sing' and 'Silent Night' and all thought of our families back at home. It all made for a very memorable festive occasion.

While we were hiding at the Prinzens' there was a constant risk of discovery, not just from the Germans but also from the Dutch fascist police, the NSB, who made several surprise inspections looking for the unregistered people they knew were hiding out on farms like the Prinzens'. These inspections were called 'Razziers' and the police would cordon off an area while they conducted their search. Small boys like Benny were briefed to cycle around the neighbourhood to give warnings if there was any sight of the NSB. These police were greatly hated and were called the 'Zwarten' ('Blacks') because of the colour of their uniforms.

One evening in January 1945, while Long Henk was visiting us, there was a knock at the door of the farmhouse and a warning from neighbours that the NSB police were carrying out a Razzier. We all ran into the barn and climbed up to our hiding place in the hayloft before the NSB arrived. After searching the farmhouse they came into the barn, shining their torches up towards our hideout. We all had our Sten guns at the ready, to defend ourselves if we were discovered. A narrow beam of torchlight threaded its way up through the gaps in the boards and shone directly on Long Henk's Luger pistol. I held my breath and tightened my grip on my gun. Fortunately for all concerned, the police below obviously could not see through into our space; the torch beam was lowered, and they completed their inspection without finding anything. Papa Prinzen helped distract the NSB by accompanying them

183

on their search and we heard him below defiantly telling them that the Tommies were soon going to be here and then they would all be hanged as traitors! I couldn't see the reaction of the NSB police but I'm sure that it distracted them.

There were also many German soldiers billeted in the neighbourhood and we were in constant danger of being discovered by them as they often came around to farmhouses in search of food. I recall one incident when we were sitting around in the Prinzens' kitchen and saw two German soldiers walk by the outside window on their way to the front door. We were able to slip out to the barn while someone in the family engaged them in conversation and sold them some food.

One might have imagined that in living at the Samsonhuis with the Prinzen family under these conditions, the worry and anxiety would be unbearable. Nothing could be further from the truth. Along with such constant tension, life at the Prinzens' farm was also a lot of fun. Truida once told me that life growing up at the farm was very boring, and nothing ever happened until our group of airmen turned up, when everything became 'fantastic'. There was constant laughter and backchat, both among ourselves and with the Dutch.

We used to run around with the Prinzen offspring, playing the children's tag game of 'He', grown men and youngsters crashing about and laughing like idiots. The young Prinzen boys were great practical jokers. The door of the toilet had a small window with a diamond-shaped hole, and the Prinzen boys would flip open the curtain that covered the window and throw in a potato, which could hit you between the eyes if you failed to take evasive action. In the winter evenings we would sit at the kitchen table, by the wood-fired stove, swapping stories and singing songs. One night we were all sitting down together; I was next to the eldest daughter, Truida, when the carbide lamp – the sole source of light – suddenly went out. While someone went off to replenish it I felt Truida's small delicate fingers push themselves into my hand. A pleasant experience for me, or so I thought. When light was restored to the darkened room I found that I was holding the hand of one of the brothers instead – he and Truida had managed to switch places without my noticing. Everyone, including Truida, thought that this was a huge joke and fell about laughing.

On another occasion we were asked by Papa Prinzen to share with them some of the Dutch words that we had learnt. The boys had taught Joe Davis a few Dutch words, but when he innocently repeated them to the parents he found that he had been taught a string of swear words, which caused great shock and embarrassment – Mother Prinzen (rather questionably I thought) claimed, 'No one learnt those words in this house.'

The Prinzens were very religious people; grace was said at every meal as we sat around the kitchen table with the family. At lunchtime a passage would be read from the Bible and one of the family would be called upon to speak aloud some Bible verses. This was probably outside the experience of most of us airmen at the time, but fortuitously I had been in the choir during my

185

schooldays. So that when we were called upon to recite a psalm I was able to recall 'Brother James's Air', the words of which are based on Psalm 23. With helpful prompting from the boys, I repeated the words and was able to do my mother proud. After the war the Prinzens and Hoftizers came to my wedding and their wedding present was a framed text from Psalm 23.

Between the airmen, the wisecracks of Bob Hope and Frank Sinatra were woven into our language, not to mention Mae West with her 'Come up and see me sometime' style, and S.J. Perelman with his 'Love is not the dying moan of a violin – it's the triumphant twang of a bedspring.' I greatly enjoyed the humour of James Thurber's books and cartoons, and Damon Runyon's tales of the New York underground and its characters such as Harry the Horse. These became entwined in our folklore. There was always a lot of banter and vulgar stories, often wildly implausible claims about the respective sexual achievements and failings of the various nationalities making up the aircrew. I remember Joe saying to Bernard, 'You've got a smile on your face, what were you up to last night with your wife?' and Bernard would take this teasing in good heart.

I got some ribbing for the romantic feelings that existed between Truida and myself. The other airmen asked me what I would do if I found Truida on my doorstep after the war. Like a gentleman I replied that I did not know and would just wait and see. In the situation that we were in, it would have been a gross betrayal of the family to behave with anything other than complete propriety towards Truida.

Then there was listening to music and singing. Even possessing a radio was forbidden, so enjoying music on the radio was limited to a few minutes before and after the all-important BBC news and sometimes the American Forces Network for a brief spell. Thus we kept abreast of the big bands of the day and the 'top of the hit parade' tunes. Glenn Miller's 'In the Mood' was a great favourite at that time, as was 'Yellow Rose of Texas'. We knew all the big bands and notable singers such as Ella Fitzgerald, Doris Day, the Ink Spots and the inimitable 'Satchmo', Louis Armstrong – all American of course, but known to us all. From the BBC we sometimes heard Vera Lynn with the 'White Cliffs of Dover' and 'We'll Meet Again', but somehow this sentimental style did not accord with our situation. Vera Lynn was an attractive young lady and a great entertainer, but when one's main concern was whether one would still be alive tomorrow, the 'White Cliffs of Dover' were not our prime concern – but 'In the Mood' did us good!

Singing played a major part in our evening entertainment. We used to sing hit songs like the 'Yellow Rose of Texas' and we were taught the Dutch words to a French marching song from the First World War about a café proprietor's daughter called Madelein. We would enthusiastically sing this with the boys at De Berk and I still remember the Dutch words today. We also sang 'It's a Long Way to Tipperary' in the original English and, of course, 'Lili Marlene.' The Dutch even taught us an old song from the Boer War about the Transvaal – they brought up the Boer War sometimes but seemed willing to forgive the British for it. So anyone passing by De Berk on a quiet evening could have been entertained by a varied programme of songs sung with great vigour in a number of languages.

Naturally, we were intensely interested in the progress of the war and interrogated newly arrived airmen on the latest news. Around Christmas we heard on the BBC news about the German offensive in the Ardennes and were very depressed; it seemed that the war in Europe would drag on even longer. In the Pacific, the capture of islands like Iwo Jima was taking place around this time, and this news was more encouraging. We also heard about attacks on British troops in Palestine by terrorist groups like the Stern gang and the Irgun Zevai Leumi. Who were these people and on which side were they fighting? There were two or three Jewish men in the resistance group based at De Berk and they were as shocked as we were by this news. It was common knowledge that people were dying of cold and hunger in the cities of Holland, and suffering terribly in the concentration camps in Germany, so every British division that could be scraped together in the Middle East was needed for the last big push across the Rhine to end the war in Europe. And yet British troops were required in Palestine to maintain order there – I still feel astonished that this was happening while the war in Europe was continuing.

On New Year's Day in 1945 the Germans launched an enormous air offensive against the

US and British forward bases in Belgium and Holland. We saw hundreds of German bombers passing overhead and realised that this was a major attack. It was quite a sombre day for us all as we became aware that the Germans could still cause a lot of damage and it was clear that the war was far from over. We saw that many of the German planes were jet fighters/bombers and wondered if there was substance in the Nazi propaganda about new weapons that would change the course of the war. I found out later that around 800 German planes took part in these raids and they had some success in destroying Allied planes on the ground, but suffered heavy losses both from their own anti-aircraft gunners (who were not expecting to see German aircraft in the sky) and from US and British fighters and anti-aircraft units. It turned out to be the last German air offensive of the war but we, of course, did not know this at the time.

There were regular USAAF daytime and RAF night-time raids passing overhead on their way to Germany. In early 1945 while bombers on a big USAAF daylight assault were flying by high above us we noticed little dots in the sky around them. After a descent of about half an hour the dots materialised as large brown paper packages that were used to contain Window to confuse German radar. In one of the packages we found a copy of the *Saturday Evening Post* that was only a week old and it was eagerly perused by us as we were starved of news from home and reading material in English. This was the only time in my stay in Holland that I was able to find something to read in English and I pounced on it. I remember that the magazine contained an Ernest Hemingway short story, *The Short Happy Life of Francis Macomber,* about big game hunting in Africa, which I enjoyed greatly as Hemingway was one of my favourite authors.

It was interesting to observe the reactions of ordinary people in Holland when the great armadas of American B17 Fortresses and B24 Liberators flew over on their way to bomb German targets in daytime. They would run out into the streets to wave them on their way and to taunt any German soldiers who might be standing near. Likewise at night, as the British Lancasters and Halifaxes rumbled overhead, people would stop and listen to the sound and nod their heads approvingly.

One of the leaders of the local resistance group, Co Hetinger, worked at an enamelware factory and was told that the Germans were going to take over the building for war production. We suspected that they were going to start using it to manufacture mines, so decided to remove the stock. Ben was sent to the factory with a horse and cart, which he loaded with enamelware such as pots and pans. He was stopped at a road-block by German soldiers who wanted to search his cart but he reeled off such a tirade of expletives that they left him alone. He arrived at the Prinzens' farm with a large enamel bath on his cart that we hooked up with pipes from the stove so we could channel hot water into the bath. The ten pairs of eyes of the Prinzen children watched us intently as we stripped off and took our first bath in months. Apparently the children wanted to see if we were built the same way as they were. It seems we were passed OK.

Chapter 18

Efforts to Return and New Arrivals

Ever since my arrival in Holland I had continued to try to find out how to link up with the British forces on the southern side of the River Rhine. I wanted to pass on what I'd seen of the mobile V2 launch and, of course, get back to my family and friends, who did not even know that I was still alive. Bob Kroll's name was occasionally mentioned in conversation between Jan, Henk and Co and one gained the impression that he was someone to whom Jan reported. In November 1944 Joe and I were visited by Bob and he took me aside for a quiet talk. He was a man of about thirty with a good command of English. He explained that prior to the German invasion in 1940 he had been a major in the Dutch Army and he had some authority in the Resistance.

Without mentioning anything about the Resistance he said that enquiries were being made on behalf of Joe and myself to see if we could be ferried across the Rhine in the vicinity of Arnhem, where there were as many as 300–400 British paratroopers still in hiding. They were proving something of an embarrassment to the civilian population, not only because of the danger involved in concealing them, but because of the difficulty in obtaining food coupons for bread and so forth. He said that it might be possible to include us with groups of men who were to be secretly ferried across the Rhine.

November came and went and nothing happened. I subsequently learnt that a large group of around 140 – largely soldiers from Operation Market Garden and also some aircrew – had successfully traversed the Rhine in Operation Pegasus I on the night of 22/23 October 1944. A second group was to be taken across the Rhine on the night of 18/19 November 1944 as part of an operation called Pegasus II. Unfortunately, after Pegasus I an irresponsible newspaper correspondent in England interviewed a survivor. Somehow the story got past the military censor and was published in a daily newspaper so the secret got out. Luckily for me I was not able to join the Pegasus II group, as they ran into a German ambush when they were about to cross the Ede–Arnhem main road and all but seven of the group were killed or captured.

After the war I found out that MI9, the British agency responsible for assisting escaping prisoners, had an officer, Airey Neave, based in Nijmegen on the south side of the Rhine. In his book *Saturday at MI9* Neave relates the work of Dick Kraght, a Dutchman working for SOE who was a leading figure in organising the escape route for soldiers hiding in the vicinity of Arnhem. Dick Kraght worked closely with an airborne officer, Major Digby Tatham-Warter. They were able to access a private telephone line between the power stations at Nijmegen and Ede on the German-occupied north side of the Rhine to get in touch with the Dutch Resistance and plan the Pegasus operations. It seems likely to me that Bob Kroll was in contact with Dick Kraght when attempting to arrange for Joe Davis and myself to be included in the next batch of those fleeing over the Rhine. During December 1944 and January 1945 we heard rumours that other escapees were being smuggled to British lines through the marshy area in the delta between the Rhine and the Maas, known as the Biesbosch. By this time Airey Neave had returned to London, his place being taken by Captains Hugh Frazer and Maurice Macmillian, who arranged the passage in small groups by canoe.

In early 1945 we heard that there was to be another attempt to cross the Rhine. We were to be put in a rowing boat near the town of Wesel higher up the river in Germany; the plan was to float down the Rhine to the southern side, which was in British hands. On 8 February 1945, the day that the escape was planned, we were all very excited at the thought that we were going to return home and the Prinzen family prepared an evening feast with a bottle of wine to mark our departure. As far as I can recall this was the only time that we drank alcohol while in hiding. Some of my Dutch friends turned out to be great drinkers after the war, but this wasn't a side of them I saw at the time. However, that night the British launched Operation Veritable, an offensive to clear the land east of Nijmegen between the Maas and Rhine Rivers. We felt and heard the bombardment commence as the ground began to shake and the drainpipes on the side of the house started rattling. We all went outside and from the farmyard we could see a bright glow in the sky from the searchlights that shone into the clouds to illuminate the attack. When the man came to collect us to join the rest of the escapees, the brilliance from the searchlights across the front ten miles away was so strong that we could read a newspaper even though it was night-time, and he told us that our flight from Holland had to be cancelled. We were all very keyed up and dreadfully disappointed not to leave, although I'm not sure whether we could have pulled it off if the escape plan had proceeded.

Another potential opportunity to return arose when Field Marshal Model, the commander of the German Army Group B, set up a new HQ at the nearby town of Doetinchem. General Student, the commander of the German airborne forces, was attached to this headquarters, and had a small Feiseler Storch plane there for personal use or reconnaissance purposes. My friend Co Hetinger was in the habit of cycling past the field where the aircraft was kept within 100 yards of the road. Through chatting to the sentry he found out that it was maintained there with a full fuel tank and ready to use at any time. We considered borrowing the plane to take us back to British lines but there were problems with fitting all of the airmen into a three-seater. Starting the aircraft would be another challenge. We were also concerned at the likely reprisals to civilians in the area if we took it, so reluctantly abandoned the idea.

Later on, towards the end of our time at Samsonhuis, when things were very bad and the danger to the family was extreme, I suggested to the other men that it would be best if we left and all took our chances in trying to get across the River Rhine to the British front line. I asked Bobby if he would accompany me. He said he would – surely a test of comradeship. Jan turned up and dissuaded us – which was probably just as well because Bobby and I knew that to traverse the river by passing through a lightly defended stretch of riverbank we would have had to enter a minefield.

In late January Jim Strickland, an Australian, was shot down over Düsseldorf, and like me set out to walk westwards from Germany to the front lines. He had an even harder time than I did and it took him nine days to trek to Holland – it was miraculous that he managed this without shelter and with very little food. Jim found travelling at night in the middle of winter very testing and he ended up walking in the daytime, wearing his navy blue 'frock' sweater over his RAF uniform to cover up his clothes and look like a local peasant. When he was so far gone that he could hardly stand, he finally made it into the town of Winterswijk, realised that he was in the Netherlands, and staggered into a baker's shop on the main street, telling them that he was a British airman. From here he was led to the Resistance who put him with us at the Prinzens' farm. Jim was a tough, well-balanced extrovert, good humoured, and like many Australians, uncomplaining in adversity and ready for anything.

On the night of 21/22 February 1945 there was a major RAF night raid on the Dortmund–Ems canal and the return route of the bombers took them over our farm. We heard the bombers overhead and came out to watch. With a medium level of cloud and a half-moon above we could observe them silhouetted against the sky. Not only could we see them but so could the German night fighters flying below the bomber stream. There must have been six to eight planes just in the sweep of the sky visible to us from the farmyard. Apparently a total of thirteen Lancasters were lost on this raid, seemingly hit by upward-firing guns from fighters flying beneath them, and each bomber burst into flames. One plane was hit, turned over, and collided with another, resulting in a huge explosion. We knew that we had just seen fourteen fellow fliers killed in that one explosion, and this was very upsetting.

The nearest of the other aircraft that were shot down fell to earth only a mile or so away and we counted five parachutes opening before the plane hit the ground. Subsequently, the Canadian pilot, Chuck Huntley, was brought to Samson-huis, helped by two local men. We went to meet them in the dark and when we asked how he was Chuck was not able to reply. He was led into the kitchen where by carbide lamplight we could see that he was badly burnt on his face, chest and hands and in great pain. I remember that his tie had left its imprint on his scorched chest.

196

Fortunately his flying goggles had saved his eyes. We peeled his clothes off carefully and gave him aspirin, the only painkiller that we had.

The next day Jan arranged for a Dutch doctor to see him. The doctor ground sulphanilamide pills (used to treat bacterial infections) – which he'd stolen from Germans that he had treated in the local hospital – into a powder that was sprinkled on to his wounds, and administered a stronger painkiller. Chuck was laid in our communal bed in the hideout and we took turns keeping watch over him and giving him drinks of water. The awful smell of his charred flesh – just like burnt pork – pervaded the place. Although he was an invalid during his time with us, he remained cheerful. Meeting Chuck in later life one would hardly know that he had been badly burnt – we did a good job in fixing him up! I believe that, except for one who was taken as a prisoner of war, the other members of his crew who parachuted out were found by German soldiers and shot. By this stage of the war German soldiers had a great hatred for the Allied airmen who were bombing them and their homeland and we knew that we could expect little mercy if we were captured.

So by February 1945 there were seven airmen hiding in the hayloft at the Prinzens' farm. For my part the Dutch tended to turn to me when opinions were sought, partly because I was the first of our group to arrive in Holland and partly because it could be seen that within the group of seven of us most of the others looked to me for whatever reason when decisions needed to be

197

made. Although I was only twenty-one, I wasn't particularly uncomfortable with this; it seemed natural in the circumstances and it was common in wartime for responsibility to be placed on young men. However, it did seem to trouble Joe and there was some underlying tension between us. All that said, we got on well together, there were no shouting matches or anger or dramatics; instead, as I have said, there was a lot of humour and laughter.

The initial excitement of my first few months in Holland seemed a long time ago as the war went on and we endured a long, bitterly cold, winter. Throughout, I was haunted by the memories of what happened when I was shot down, and what may have been Ron's fate. I was not in any way overwhelmed by such thoughts running through my head, but it was a constant nagging emotional pain. I grieved for my family, and what they were imagining about me, while on top of everything else I continually speculated on how it was all going to end. Because of my involvement with the Resistance and their activities I frequently thought about how I would stand up to torture if I fell into German hands. I didn't talk about my inner feelings with the other airmen but I'm sure that they were similarly affected.

Living conditions that winter were very tough and we had to improvise in order to provide ourselves with the basics. I made a comb using Perspex salvaged from a bomber and a buckle for my belt from the butt plate of a broken .303 rifle. In February it was bitterly cold. Our bedding at the Prinzens' consisted of two blankets sewn end to end that just stretched across one bedspace, a vast heavy riding cloak, and a rather thin German Army greatcoat. We went to bed fully clothed every night. Beneath us we had 2 inches of straw. Above us we looked up at the underside of the roof tiles, which sloped from a height of about 6 feet near the entrance door to the hiding place to about 4 feet 6 inches by the outer wall. By propping up a tile on, say a matchbox, one gained a view of the countryside through the aperture.

The snow would make its way through gaps in the tiled roof where we slept and I often remember having a light dusting of snow lying all over our bedding. I got very ill at this time. The German Army had brought lice with it from its stay on the Eastern Front and anyone who had been directly, or indirectly, in contact with German soldiers would get lice themselves. I spent two days at the home of Co Hetinger, in order to reconnoitre General Student's headquarters and the location of his aircraft. Co had previously had German soldiers billeted with him, and I got lice, which in turn I passed on to the other airmen. I scratched away to get rid of the lice and these scratches became infected. I was soon suffering from septicaemia, and in my fever experienced very high temperatures; I was told later that I was delirious although I was not aware of this at the time. The top of my head was so badly infected that it became swollen and soft. My sleeping place was moved to the far side of the communal bed so that I wouldn't contaminate the others and I was so ill that I thought I would die. The local doctor was brought in to look at me and he gave me some of the sulphanilamide tablets he had stolen from the Germans and these new drugs cleared up the infection. Tragically, the doctor was killed shortly afterwards when a British Typhoon shot up his car as he was visiting other patients.

While I was lying sick in bed I heard the boys downstairs laughing and then the sounds of some-one coming up the ladder that led to our hiding space. I was astonished to see two uniformed German soldiers come up the ladder through the door, calling out 'Hello Frank' to me. It turned out that they were two deserters from the German Army who originally came from Alsace-Lorraine, part of France that was reabsorbed into the German Reich after the invasion in 1940. My mates had thought it was funny to send them up in their uniforms to see me, but in my ill and feverish state this episode had a nightmarish quality. It gave me a real fright and I might easily have shot them with my Mauser had I not realised from the laughter that they were not a real threat.

Later in February a German officer and ser-geant came to the Prinzens' farm to buy food. We airmen had just killed a pig and because it was necessary for farmers to closely account for all livestock we needed to dispose of its meat before the Germans came back the next day. We spent the whole night cooking the pig, making sausages and putting fat in a storage box. I found killing the pig an exceptionally brutal process; I offered to shoot the pig to give it a more humane death but was dissuaded from doing so. The experience did not make me long for the bucolic pleasures of rural life.

This visit brought home to me that the front line was very close and there was a strong probability that there would be German soldiers billeted at the farmhouse in the near future. If there were enemy soldiers around, how would we get food or hand down a toilet bucket? The hayloft ran along one side of the barn with the central part clear to the roof. The loft had six or more doors in the tongued-and-grooved panelling above the cattle stalls, through which hay could be dropped. A further door had had its hinges removed and made to match the panelling. This was the entrance to our hiding place but it required a ladder to get up and down. I decided that we needed another means of going in and out; in retrospect this was the most important decision I made during my time in Holland.

I asked Papa Prinzen for a hammer and chisel and we set to work to cut through the floorboards, following the line of the nails above the joists, and cut out a trapdoor some 18 x 24 inches square. This created an entry and exit from our hiding place to a small washhouse room below. Directly beneath the trapdoor there was a large stone sink that one could climb down to, and beside the sink was the pump, the main water supply for the house. The position of the pump meant that it could only be worked with the access door to the house closed, so if someone tried opening the door while the pump was being operated they would graze the knuckles of the person using it. This gave the Prinzens an excuse to lock the door to the washroom, which proved to be very useful for us. The ceiling of the washhouse was relatively low, so a tray could be handed up or a bucket lowered reasonably easily – we had a practice session with the Prinzen family to make sure that this could be done without risk of discovery.

We latched the original entrance up to the hide-out on the inside so that it could not be opened and moved the ladder beneath it to another location in the barn to ensure that there was no clue to where the original entrance was located. I felt that we were at least prepared for closer scrutiny by the Germans but a secure hiding place would not necessarily save us if the Prinzens' farmhouse became part of the front line when the Allied offensive across the Rhine finally started.

Chapter 19

The German Soldiers at De Berk

One evening at the beginning of March 1945 there was an urgent knocking on the back door of Samsonhuis. A partisan from De Berk had a message from Jan for Joe and myself to come at once to their farm as they had captured four Germans and Jan wanted to discuss what was to be done. There was also a request for Bernard Prinzen to find a long rope and take it there. Joe and I at once appreciated the seriousness of the situation – how on earth could we keep any German prisoners? I took off my workman's overalls and put on my uniform (such as it was) and officer's forage cap. I felt that it was important to conduct things in a proper military fashion; I suppose that I wanted to appear to the Dutch and Germans as a serving soldier.

We set off for De Berk, telling the rest of our group to follow. Bernard trailed behind us carrying the rope and in an uncharacteristically excited frame of mind, perhaps not realising the grave circumstances we were in and the sinister implications of the request for rope.

We arrived at De Berk and in the dim light of an oil lamp found a German lieutenant and three soldiers lined up facing the barn wall, with a partisan holding a Sten gun at the ready three or four paces behind each of them. The Germans had their arms tied behind their backs and were gagged. Their execution looked to be imminent, so I immediately stepped between the prisoners and their guards in an effort to delay any shooting until we had a chance to speak to Jan. The German lieutenant was a scholarly looking man of about thirty, with horn-rimmed spectacles. In civilian life I could picture him as a junior partner in a firm of country solicitors. He caught my eye and looked at me with great interest – he would have been able to see from my uniform that I was a British serviceman. I felt his life was in my hands.

Jan was upstairs looking at the Germans' documents and came down to us when he heard that we had arrived. When he saw where I was standing he was furious and with his Colt 45 gun in hand he ordered me away from the Germans. Together with Joe we went back upstairs to a room with a table that he used as his office. Putting his Colt 45 on the table, and still irate, Jan said, 'We have been helping you, now you must help us. We cannot keep these men as prisoners and they must die.'

I had never seen Jan so angry with me and I felt his words very deeply. I knew that we were completely in Jan's debt for everything that he'd done, putting his own life at risk on numerous occasions for the sake of the aircrew. Nevertheless, I could not stand by and see these men executed. I said something about the Geneva Convention.

He replied: 'And what mercy would you expect from them in your situation with civilian clothes and carrying a gun yourself?'

Of course there was no answer to this. I asked why the Germans were there – were they looking for partisans or aircrew, or rounding up young men for labour work? Had it leaked out that the Resistance was using De Berk as a base? Jan pointed to the paybooks and wallets that had been taken from the Germans, which were spread out on the table. It appeared that they came from a standard infantry unit, so perhaps they were just earmarking buildings that could be used as billets or where field guns or armoured vehicles could be hidden. They had said nothing during interrogation.

Later, Henk told me what had happened when the Germans turned up at De Berk. Jan and Henk and the rest of the partisans had been alerted to their arrival and hid upstairs in total silence. The lieutenant and his sergeant forced their way into the building through its side doors and looked around. Suddenly something aroused their suspicion (Henk thought that it might have been the smell of cooking or the sound of a Sten gun being cocked) and abruptly they ran out of the building. Henk and a group of partisans sprinted after them in pursuit. They first captured the lieutenant and sergeant, and then carefully went out to the road where they found and took prisoner the driver and another soldier waiting in an Opel car.

I picked up the wallet belonging to the lieutenant and on opening it immediately saw a charming photograph of a beautiful blonde girl in her late twenties holding the hands of two young boys aged about six or seven years. What could I do to prevent this man being executed?

In my experience of warfare, when one armed man confronts his enemy, also armed, you kill him before he kills you and it is an impersonal event. But when you are aware of his family and children it becomes very different. In cold blood, it becomes murder. This is what I then had to face.

Was there any alternative? I wanted to stop the execution but couldn't think of any way of avoiding the necessity for it. We had no means for holding the Germans prisoner, particularly with the increased military activity in the area that was likely to result from the Allied offensive, which we knew to be imminent. I argued with Jan for five minutes or so but I could not suggest a practical alternative. It was late at night and we knew that these men would soon be missed from their unit; we had to make a decision quickly. There was no time for a protracted argument or discussion. They must die. I felt strongly that they should at least be treated as military men so I suggested that as soldiers they should be shot. But Jan was concerned that the sounds of gunfire would be heard by others in the vicinity.

I went back downstairs and found that the other airmen had arrived and were standing in the doorway. We gathered together and I put it to them that we would take no part in the execution of the Germans and instead help to dispose of the bodies. I was torn. I still resisted the necessity of the execution but I felt strongly that we had to help our Dutch friends in some way. This was agreed to by the other airmen. The atmosphere at De Berk seemed grotesque to me. Some of the Resistance fighters appeared excited and pleased at the prospect of the executions; no one looked to be as dismayed by what was happening as I was. I suppose that this was because the Dutch – and to an even greater extent the Poles in our group – had such an intense hatred of the Germans as a result of the many terrible things they had done during the occupation of their countries. Great Britain never had to endure such an experience so it was not for us to judge how we might have acted had we been in their shoes.

The prisoners were led down into the cellar of the barn. The rope brought by Bernard had been thrown over a beam in the roof of the barn itself and Joe, presumably drawing on his experience with the Ku Klux Klan, tied a hangman's knot at one end. Each prisoner was brought from the cellar in turn, had the noose placed around their neck, and was required to climb up the ladder. Then the ladder was kicked away to hang the prisoner. This was not a very effective technique and did not kill them instantly. Instead they slowly strangled. I was sickened. Joe very coolly took the pulse of each prisoner to confirm that they were dead.

I felt obliged to watch what was happening, and with the others I soon had to focus on what we would do about assisting with the bodies. This was going to be a challenge as we were acutely aware that any evidence of an attack by the Resistance on German soldiers was likely to provoke reprisals on the local civilian population on the most appalling scale, so needed to make sure nothing pointed to its involvement.

We thought of simply burying the bodies in some farmer's field, but the innocent farmer would inevitably get the blame if they were dis-covered and we would still be left with the sol-diers' small Opel car to dispose of. We considered pushing the car into a river but didn't know how deep the local river was and whether we could successfully submerge it. Yet it was imperative to act quickly that night and come up with a plan that we could immediately implement. At this time Allied intruder aircraft were regularly patrolling the main roads at night, attacking German vehicles, so I decided that we would try to blow up the Germans in their Opel on a main road in a way that would simulate such an air strike.

The loading of the soldiers into the Opel proved

a problem. In our initial attempts to lift the first individual we found it nearly impossible. If we tried to drag him by hauling on his jacket collar, with all the body's muscular strength gone the jacket just slipped off. So we rolled each body on to a ladder that we used as a stretcher and four of us carried it to the car, where, with great difficulty, we eventually loaded all four corpses on to the back seat. Apart from the physical effort, the smell was appalling, as at the moment of death all the muscles of the bodies had relaxed, including the rectum, so they were covered with excrement. I was nauseated by the task. To add to the horror of the situation, one of the Germans appeared to groan as we carried him out to the car. Quickly one of the Poles stepped forward with a knife to cut his throat to make sure that life was extinguished. The Pole was restrained, but there were no further groans anyway.

The materials air dropped to the Resistance included blocks of 'Drottil' dynamite intended to be used for cutting steel constructions like railway lines or bridges. We placed these explosive charges on the floor of the Opel, together with a German 'panzerfaust' rocket that the Resistance boys had somehow acquired. We also had slow- and fast-burning fuses that led to detonators. I started putting together a mixture of fuses in such a way that all of them would detonate at the same time. Joe interrupted me and testily said that there was no need to put multiple fuses in place – the manual said one fuse and the detonator would do the job. The atmosphere was already on edge, so rather than have a ridiculous argument or stand-up fight, I reluctantly did as Joe suggested.

We needed to get the car to a nearby stretch of straight road where it would be plausible for it to have been destroyed in an attack by night-intruder aircraft. The group at De Berk included the two German Army deserters from Alsace-Lorraine, and one of these men – no doubt hoping to prove his worth among us – volunteered to drive the Opel. With Long Henk in charge, the two of them sat in the front seats and drove off towards the main road between Aalten and Doetinchem, which we had identified as a plausible site for an air attack. However, driving along a narrow country lane with steep banks on either side, they encountered a German Army bus that almost blocked the road. Its passengers, German soldiers, were standing around having a smoke and a break. The Alsatian put his foot down on the accelerator, and with its wheels running along the bank, the Opel squeezed through the group of soldiers, scattering them, and just managed to get past the bus.

Unnerved by this narrow escape, Long Henk decided to drive on for just another mile before he and the driver stopped the Opel and lit the fuse to blow up the car. Long Henk reported to me that although the Opel caught fire and burnt furiously, there was no big explosion, so I suspect that the panzerfaust and car's fuel tank may have ignited but there wasn't a proper detonation of the explosive charges. The nature of the explosive was perhaps also not ideal; I was told later that Drottil dynamite creates a heat intense enough to melt railway lines but not a great explosive blast.

At any event there was not an eruption sufficient to destroy all the evidence of what had happened, and I bitterly regretted that I'd allowed Joe to cut short my preparation of the fuses.

We realised that the Germans would come looking for the missing soldiers, so that same night all the men quartered at De Berk and the seven airmen were led to a grain store on the Aalten–Dinxperlo road, near a windmill. I was surprised to see that while food was desperately short, there must have been thirty to forty sacks of wheat waiting to be milled. We used these to make a firing position inside the main door and to make fire steps inside the windows at each end. Men were posted armed with Bren guns and rifles, while more than twenty of us hid in the space under the floor (which was some 4 feet above the ground for ease of loading the sacks). There we tried to get a little sleep as we awaited developments.

The next morning we emerged from below the floor to continue guarding the grain store, while Jan and several others slipped out to find farms willing to hide some of our group of thirty. In the middle of the morning we heard the sound of soldiers marching along the road. Peering out of the window on that side of the grain store we saw a platoon of about thirty German soldiers; behind them was a captured British 1,500-cwt Army truck carrying the soldiers' heavy kit. What was extraordinary was that the truck was pulled by a farm horse, with a man at the steering wheel guiding it, suggesting that there was no petrol available. To our dismay the platoon halted outside our grain store. We could hear their conversation through the door and even smell their cigarette smoke as they sat around resting their feet. We all 'stood to', as the military say, with our guns at the ready in case any were too inquisitive and we had no option but to emerge from our hiding place and start shooting. After a very long thirty minutes they reassembled and departed, horse-truck and all.

Towards nightfall Jan returned, having had a difficult time. The word had got around that there had been trouble and that hostages had been taken. Farmers and householders were understandably terrified about giving shelter to the likes of us. However, some did, and those remarkable people the Prinzen family agreed to take us back at Samsonhuis, but on condition that we remained totally confined in the small hiding place in the hayloft. This we readily agreed to. So at about 8 p.m. we returned to Samsonhuis in the darkness and once again were warmly welcomed by the Prinzens. All this had happened within a few days of leaving my sickbed and I arrived back mentally and physically exhausted. The awfulness of recent events bore down heavily upon me and all I wanted to do was sleep. I remember the eldest daughter, Truida, asking me how things had been and in my halting Dutch I replied that it had been, quite simply, murder.

The final outcome of the killing of the soldiers was as grim as we feared. Because the car had been blown up before reaching a main road there was clearly no possibility of it and the bodies being viewed as the result of an air attack; instead the Germans instantly realised that the four soldiers had been put to death by the Resistance. They at once set about reprisals and took some forty-five prisoners from the jail at Doetinchem to a field near the scene of the explosion and forced them to dig a large pit before they were shot on the spot and buried. There is now a memorial called Monument Varsseveld, 'Aaltense Tol', erected to mark the scene of the executions. It has a sealed glass receptacle containing wheat from the field. The inscription on the memorial states, 'Warm blood soaked our fields and the crop grew richer', alluding to the fact that wheat from the section of the field where the men were buried grew higher than elsewhere on the land.

This tragic episode left a feeling of some animosity in the neighbourhood towards the Resistance. People were appalled by what had happened and were reluctant to give shelter to the Resistance fighters involved. As the local resistance group commander, Jan must have felt this acutely and he told me that after the war ended he had not felt able to go back to Aalten, where he had many friends, for ten years.

From my own perspective I did not dwell on Jan's angry reaction towards my intervention. However, I did in part hold him responsible for what had happened, and thought that he might have found some other way of dealing with the fate of the four Germans. I now believe this judgement was unfair to Jan; there were no obvious alternatives, such as keeping them prisoner, and I believe he did not take the decision lightly.

In many respects it took much courage on Jan's part to arrive at that difficult conclusion. I felt a great deal of empathy for the German lieutenant and his men – like so many others in the war, they were probably just ordinary men in the wrong place at the wrong time.

Chapter 20

A Final Test and Liberation

Shortly after we'd returned to Samsonhuis and our hiding place, a truck turned up at the farmstead with a platoon of about twenty German parachutists. A lieutenant and sergeant were billeted in the farmhouse and the rest of the unit were allocated to our barn and an adjacent building. A 1,500-cwt truck was parked in the barn directly under our hideout and the driver and some of the men appeared to be sleeping in it. On the first night of their stay, having settled in and had an early evening meal in an outbuilding, the lieutenant sat down at the harmonium in the front parlour of the house and from our hayloft we could hear the incongruous sounds of the Dutch national anthem! No doubt it was his way of ingratiating himself with the family, and perhaps a reflection that at least some Germans knew that they had lost the war, but to us hiding above this was a most extraordinary occurrence.

Several of the soldiers played other instruments, such as an accordion, trumpet and clarinet. During their stay there was an occasion

213

when some of them, keeping warm with the family in the kitchen, brought out their instruments and began to play. The musicians in the kitchen were accompanied by the lieutenant in the parlour with the harmonium, and played popular tunes in concert, 'Lili Marlene' being one. The Prinzens joined in with gusto, and even we in the barn sang it softly under our breath.

During the day the Germans were busy in the neighbourhood, building trenches and gun positions, but at night they were in very close proximity to us, only a few feet below us in the barn. We could hear them chatting in the kitchen of the house, which was adjacent to part of the barn loft where we were hidden. We understood that they would be able to hear us as easily as we heard them so we had to remain completely silent to avoid giving ourselves away. Bobby Brown had developed a cough and we were terrified the Germans would hear him. We took turns staying awake when he was asleep to make sure that he didn't cough loudly in his slumber and once, when the Germans were immediately underneath us, we had to stop him coughing by stuffing his head in a pillow. He told me afterwards that he thought he was going to be suffocated.

The trapdoor that we had cut in the floor proved a godsend, as we could use it to haul up food and lower down the toilet bucket without the Germans' knowledge. Bizarre though the situation was, we derived some comfort from the thought that the last place the Germans would think of finding us, would be in their own billet.

The Germans did not notice that the Prinzens

were cooking twice as much food as would have been required for the needs of the family and the billeted soldiers. Somehow, the Prinzens managed to slip into the washroom to hand us up food and pass the toilet bucket up or down. Pretending to operate the pump gave them the excuse for their visits and by locking the door they prevented any of the Germans inadvertently stumbling in on what they were doing.

Naturally, it was an awful strain for us living in such a confined space and also avoiding any activity that could make a sound that the Germans might hear. Time passed very slowly and one continually thought: How will it all end? We had our Sten guns hanging up on nails and didn't have any specific plan, but certainly intended to resist if we were discovered. Time dragged on and we played paper games like noughts and crosses, and battleships, to help pass the time. Our American allies taught me to play poker and we would engage in this during the day, but not at night when the Germans were about. The Americans kept a ledger of debts, which Joe took very seriously, and of course I didn't often come out ahead. It was later agreed that all outstanding debts would be cancelled, which was very fortunate for me otherwise I'd still be paying them off!

Extraordinarily, Jan contrived to come and visit us in the early hours of the morning on one occasion. He managed to avoid the Germans sleeping beneath us in the barn by crawling through a pigsty at the side of the building that gave access to the washroom, and we were astonished to hear him tapping on our trapdoor to be let in. He had come to check that we were OK and to reassure us that the rest of the resistance group had also avoided detection. While I was in Holland Jan didn't lose anyone from his resistance group, a remarkable achievement in the circumstances.

The situation was stressful for us, but it must have been even more difficult for the Prinzens and their children. We had a close call one day when Benny, the youngest of the Prinzen children, innocently told a German soldier that they had fliers overhead. Fortunately, Truida heard him say this and explained it away as a reference to the planes in the sky overhead. This might not have sounded like a convincing explanation of Benny's statement, but no doubt it would have seemed more plausible to the Germans than the truth that they had Allied airmen a few feet above them. There was another incident when Bernard knocked on the trapdoor and handed us up a magazine that he thought came from a Sten gun that one of us had left behind downstairs. An hour later he knocked on the trapdoor again and asked to have the magazine back – in fact it had come from the Schmeisser submachine gun of one of the German paratroopers, who was now in trouble with his sergeant for having lost it. We handed the magazine back down and Bernard was able to restore it to its owner without anyone suspecting anything untoward.

On 21 March 1945 the British and Canadian forces crossed the Rhine at Wesel some twenty miles from us and, as we could tell by the sound of gunfire, slowly advanced in our direction. This was the moment that we had been waiting for –

and also dreading – as we knew the risks we would face if the Prinzen farmstead became part of the front line between the two armies. We could hear the differing sounds of the British 25-pounders and the German high-velocity 88-mm guns. For a couple of days the shells from British artillery seemed to be landing in our vicinity and we saw a nearby farmhouse lose its roof to gun-fire. We knew that if the Prinzen farmhouse was hit our prospects of survival would not be good. The fear of being fired at by artillery shells was great, but the threat of discovery by the Germans below was even more terrifying.

Once a day we would hear an extraordinary and terrifying noise – a rapid series of explosions that sounded like machine-gun fire except with artillery shells. Later, after liberation, we saw areas that had been completely flattened after being subjected to bombardment, with rockets fired by the British 'mattress' rocket launcher with multiple tubes (a weapon copied from the Russians).

While the British offensive approached, the German soldiers continued to occupy the farmhouse and we became worried that they intended to use it as a strongpoint and defend it to the last. On 28 March I was able to look out through gaps in the tiles in the roof to see British 25-pounder shells landing on the nearby main road, creating a jet of fire 20-30 yards long. It would have been a cruel irony to have been killed by gunfire from our own side in the last stages of the war. The Prinzen family had taken shelter in the cellar of the farmhouse, which was propped up with lengths of timber to support the ceiling in case of collapse. Somehow Bernard continued to visit us each day with food.

Then early on the morning of 29 March there was a knock on the trapdoor and Bernard told us that the Germans had all gone during the night and taken their truck with them. He said he had seen a Tommy tank down the road. We were elated and relieved. But there was no outward celebration as it was difficult to comprehend that the great moment of liberation had arrived.

So we clambered out of our hiding place and Joe Davis, Jim Strickland and I walked a quarter of a mile to the nearest main road, and then another quarter of a mile down this road, before we found an armoured car. We were able to confirm that it was British but, with a 6-pounder gun traversing around and appearing to point in our direction, we were hesitant about approaching the vehicle and didn't want to be mistaken for hostile Germans. We gingerly approached it with our hands in the air, trying to look as un-Germanlike as possible. By this time the shelling in the vicinity had ceased.

The occupants of the armoured car did not appear to have noticed us so we walked right up to it and banged on the side to get their attention. A steel hatch opened and a heavily moustached man poked his head out. I said, 'I'm Dell, we're aircrew in hiding and would be glad of assistance to get home.'

He replied, 'Jolly good show' (he was from a Guards regiment!) and called up his HQ on his radio. And so we were 'liberated' in this rather farcical fashion.

A DUKW amphibious vehicle was dispatched to pick us up, after which we were driven back to the farm – this was harder than we anticipated as we were so used to making the journey in darkness that initially we were disorientated and could not find the way back in the daylight. We had to stop at a local farm and ask for directions to the Prinzens' farm. When we eventually arrived back, the Prinzen family emerged from the cellar and we were given only fifteen minutes to say goodbye to the people who had risked their lives hiding us, before we had to leave. We had become part of the family so this was a very hard and emotional parting.

The DUKW took us on a pontoon bridge over the Rhine and handed us over to another unit. We met up with Jan, who was attired in a semimilitary uniform like nothing I had ever seen before. He was wearing German jackboots, riding breeches, an American-style leather jacket with an elaborate arrangement of straps connected to his belt, and, of course, his usual Colt 45 and Breton yachting cap. We were able to introduce Jan to the British battalion headquarters and within a couple of weeks the resistance group of about ninety men that Jan led was incorporated into a Canadian division, branching off to liberate the remainder of Holland.

We were taken on to Tilburg where I was inter-rogated by Military Intelligence along with the other airmen. I was concerned about what to say of the events at De Berk, which had led to the taking of the hostages at Aalten, and their subsequent execution. Before we were questioned I put it to the others that we should say nothing unless specifically asked. I do not think that this was driven by our avoidance of responsibility for what had happened. Rather, it was that these were local people who had died and there was bound to be a local inquiry before the dust settled and it would be unfortunate if the British military intervened prematurely.

The interrogation was conducted in a hurried fashion. I was the first to be questioned of the seven airmen and all the interviews were completed in the space of a morning. In the main, the examination followed a standard form, asking where I had been shot down; who had helped me; could I give their addresses, and so on. There was a specific question that I considered carefully: had I witnessed any atrocity? I felt able to answer this in the negative as what happened at De Berk was not an atrocity, but unavoidable, and I had not witnessed the German retribution. At the end of my interview little had been said about our involvement with the local resistance group and the help they gave us.

At the conclusion of the form filling, and bearing in mind that there were seven of us to be dealt with that morning, my interrogator said something along the lines of 'I think you are to be congratulated, you have done well; in fact if you had come back two or three weeks earlier I would have put you up for a medal. However, there are so many of you coming out of the woodwork that we simply have no time for that now.' Considering that my Mosquito was made of plywood, I thought that was a particularly apt turn of phase as it happened.

I have a copy of the report sent on to Lieutenant Colonel J.M. Langley at MI9 reporting that our group of airmen were safe, unscathed and in friendly hands, and with a list of the people like the Prinzens who I had stayed with. When I was shot down my parents were told by the Air Ministry that I was missing and they had not subsequently received any further news about me – the presumption was that I had been killed. At Tilburg I was handed a telegraph form and swiftly sent a telegram to my family saying that I was all right.

After a few days Jim, Chuck and I were flown back to RAF Northolt on the outskirts of London, while the Americans were taken off to Paris. So there was another emotional farewell and we all wrote down our home addresses on a piece of paper so that we could keep in touch.

Back in London I faced another round of interrogation, this time by MI9 at its establishment in Hall Road, Regent's Park. Like that at Tilburg this questioning largely concentrated on the circumstances of my aircraft being shot down. Once again I gave details of the Dutch people who had helped me and the events at De Berk did not arise. The upshot of this process is that there is no official British record of my involvement with the Dutch Resistance. After the war ended I was awarded a medal, not by the British Government, but by the Dutch Government for having participated with the Dutch Resistance. I was one of only eighteen foreigners who were given this decoration, called the 'Verzetsherden-kingskruis'. I also received an invitation from Prince Bernhard, who had been head of the Dutch Resistance, to meet with him at the Dutch Royal Palace at Soestdijk.

While I was in London, I sent my family another brief telegram saying that I would be home in a day or two. My parents never received the initial telegram sent from Tilburg, so when the second, laconic, telegram from London arrived, it was a great shock to them to get notification for the first time that I was still in the land of the living. I took the train to Southwick and began walking towards my parents' house. Halfway across the village green I saw my father in the distance striding in my direction, presumably heading for a train or bus to his office in Brighton. He saw me when we were a couple of hundred yards away and we hastened to throw our arms around one another with tears in our eyes.

'Where are you off to?' I asked.

'Well we got your telegram two days ago,' he replied, 'so we knew you were alive after all this time, but these two days have been the longest of my life because I was so afraid that you might be coming back maimed or disabled. I was popping into the office for an hour or two to take these thoughts out of my mind.'

Within ten minutes I was home, with my mother's arms around me and tears running freely.

When we were all composed they naturally wanted to know what had happened to me and where I had been for the six months I had been posted as missing. This prompted me to remember the green form that I had had to sign when interrogated by MI9 in London, saying that under no circumstances should one disclose any information about my escape and evasion in case it should be of value to the enemy. When I was bursting to tell them everything this was very hard. I did, however, give my mother a pair of miniature wooden shoes – and a wink! It was not until the war ended officially on 8 May 1945 that I was able to tell my family that I had been living in Holland for six months and the whole story came flooding out.

Chapter 21

My Life after the War

After a few days with my family I went back to my old 692 Squadron and found that there was no one there that I knew from my previous service. All my contemporaries had completed their tour of operations – averaging two to three operations per week one could comfortably finish a tour of forty-five operations within six months. The new CO said that there was no point in staying with the squadron as it was about to be disbanded, there being no call for a Mosquito squadron in the Far East where the war was continuing. I felt that I had done my bit on the front line and asked to join a transport squadron so I could keep flying. I was posted to 52 Squadron at Dum Dum, Calcutta, India, to fly Dakotas (DC3s). Before I was sent out east I was dispatched to a RAF camp in Norfolk for a month, where I attended lectures and participated in physical training, playing a lot of sport. I realise now that during this period I was being observed for any signs of what is now termed as post-traumatic stress disorder. Anyone identified as suffering from this would be sent on what we knew as a 'bow and arrow' course – so called because of the time spent on archery – to recover.

After six months in the Far East my demob date came up, and no decision had been made on the application for a permanent commission that I had made back in 1944. I had the option of signing up for a further two years of service but thought that I might miss out on opportunities in civilian life, so I left the RAF in 1946 and joined British European Airways (BEA). I was based in Northolt in 1947 and married my wife Isabel that year. In 1948, BEA sent me out to fly from Cyprus and shortly after I arrived there the RAF contacted me and offered me the permanent commission that I'd been hoping for back in 1946. I decided to stick with civilian life, a decision I never regretted. I was in Cyprus until 1954 and continued to work for BEA in the UK, flying Viscounts, Vanguards and Tridents, and ultimately retiring in 1976 as British Airways' Chief Pilot (Technical). I subsequently continued to work for British Airways as a consultant, served as a member of the Board of the Civil Aviation Authority from 1982 to 1987, and served as Master of the Guild of Air Pilots and Air Navigators of London in 1988–89.

Involvement in the Escaping Society

During the war various escape lines were formed to pass airmen who had been shot down over Occupied Europe from safe house to safe house, until they reached neutral or Allied territory.

At the end of the hostilities the commander of MI9, Brigadier Norman Crockatt, compiled a report on the work of MI9 that estimated that over 33,000 escapers and evaders had passed through the hands of MI9. Of these, around 3,630 were airmen from the RAF and another 3,647 were from the USAAF.[12] These numbers were reported to the British Chiefs of Staff, and the value of the contribution of those 'helpers' in Occupied Europe, who had made possible the great escape and evasion enterprise, must have been appreciated for an awards bureau was established to acknowledge their contribution.

Certificates of Merit were issued and distributed to as many individuals as could be identified as having aided our men. The certificates were signed by Air Chief Marshal Sir Arthur Tedder, who was Chief of the Air Staff after the war. I understand that some 14,000 of these certificates were issued on behalf of RAF men alone and this was probably only the tip of the iceberg in terms of numbers. Today, many a house in Europe will have a 'Tedder Certificate' displayed with pride on the wall of the living room or kitchen.

Among the Chiefs of Staff, Lord Charles Portal, who had been Chief of the Air Staff during the war, was greatly troubled by the cost in human life and suffering of those civilians who had brought about this outcome. So many had been executed by the Germans, sent to concentration camps, and tortured for information. In 1946 Lord Portal instigated the formation of the RAF Escaping Society to maintain contact with those civilian helpers who had survived the war. To show that the RAF meant business, the Escaping Society was formed with himself as President and Sir Basil Embry, a former escaper and later Commander-in-Chief of Fighter Command, as Chairman. The RAF also provided a senior officer to serve on its otherwise civilian committee, an accountant, and an office where it could conduct its business. Financially it had to stand on its own two feet.

MI9 handed over its documents to the Escaping Society and it had records of about 14,000 civilians in Occupied Europe who had helped airmen. The information provided by MI9 enabled the Escaping Society to write to each airman who had evaded capture or later escaped from captivity and had passed through MI9's hands in the course of the war. All were invited to become members, and about 800, including myself, agreed to join. The French established a similar body called the Union Nationale des Evades de Guerre (UNEG) and it was suggested that the two associations merged. Characteristically we British declined to join our continental friends in a single organisation, but later the Escaping Society always worked closely with UNEG.

The Escaping Society endeavored to maintain contact with and to watch over the thousands of people like the Prinzen family who had helped our men, often under most perilous circumstances. From time to time the RAF provided transport aircraft to ferry helpers to Britain for visits and for us to travel to the continent in return.

The predominant concern of the Escaping Society was to raise money for the welfare of the helpers, especially those who were struggling financially, such as families whose fathers had been executed by the Germans or individuals who were in poor health. We had representatives in each country who were able to provide assistance to hard-up helpers or at least contact social services people in their own countries to see if they could intervene in needy cases. An extraordinary network of activities were coordinated through the Escaping Society's office, ranging from such matters as paying for false teeth for the widow of an elderly helper in France, to invitations for those from the continent to be guests at RAF stations or at garden parties at Buckingham Palace. The helpers tended to be older than the airmen, so as they aged later in the history of the Escaping Society it became difficult for older ones to visit the UK and instead we held functions in cities like Brussels and Paris on the continent.

Over fifty years the Escaping Society had several secretaries who played a vital role in assisting the helpers. Special mention should be made of the last and longest serving of them all, Elizabeth Harrison, as she had quite exceptional qualities. Born in Germany between the wars, her Jewish background meant her family were obliged to flee with the rise of Hitler, first to Holland, then to Belgium, and then on to Vichy France, as they attempted to stay one step ahead of the Germans in 1940. What a background for dealing with a group of people who had so much in common with her experience in trying to keep in advance of the 'nacht und nebel' (night and fog) measures that the Nazis used to make their opponents disappear without trace.

I joined the Escaping Society at its formation and became a member of its committee when I returned to the UK from Cyprus in the mid-1950s. Apart from the occasional break because of work commitments, I remained involved in the organisation until it closed down in 1995, and I had the great privilege of being its last Chairman. To this day I am indebted to the Dutch people who assisted me and feel they received scarce recognition for what they had done. The Escaping Society had little capital to dispense to help people who had sacrificed so much themselves, but it was at least satisfying to be able to bring people to events in the UK to thank them. I met some remarkable people like Dede de Jong, who with her father set up the Comet line; she was an elegant and delightful person with a strong personality and I can't speak highly enough of her.

New Information
I had always assumed my Mosquito was shot

down by anti-aircraft gunfire from the ground. However, in about 1975 I was contacted by Chris Goss, a squadron leader in the RAF who happened to live in Marlow where I also resided. He told me that he had access to Luftwaffe documents and could tell me what record they had of my aircraft if I could inform him where and when I was shot down. I provided him with this information and a few hours later he came back with the details of my aircraft and told me that a German Messerschmitt Bf110 fighter had attacked and brought down my Mosquito. This was the first intimation I had that I'd been shot down by a fighter.

At the time, the Germans were using a technique called 'Wilde Sau' (Wild Boar) for directing fighters on to the bomber streams using radar-equipped aircraft and then relying on sight – aided by searchlights and flares as well as the glow from bombing fires – to enable the fighters to cut off the bombers. We thought that our Mosquitoes were too fast to be intercepted by fighters but I now understand the Germans were able to boost the speed of their fighters to enable them to catch us. I know very little about the pilot of the Messerschmitt, Hans Durscheid, other than that he started his air force career as a flak gunner. He died only a few days after he shot me down, in a landing accident on 25 October 1944 at Köln Bonn Airport.

This new information has enabled me to reconstruct the sequence of events around being brought down. I now believe that what happened was that the elevators on the tail were shattered by gunfire from the fighter. This caused the control column to thrash to and fro and for the nose to pitch up into a stall and go into a spin. At the time I was confused by my loss of control over the aircraft and I had no ability to piece together this sequence of events.

Chapter 22

Other Post-war Histories

Ron Naiff

Ron Naiff's mother had been corresponding with my own since we both went missing in October 1944. When I returned to England in 1945 I wrote and asked if I could call on her at their family home in the Midlands. I suggested a particular day for my visit and when I knocked at the door it was answered by a man in his thirties who turned out to be Ron's elder brother. He was a Colonial Service district officer in Malaya who had been taken prisoner by the Japanese and had only recently returned from the Far East. We sat down over a cup of tea and I told him my story. Ron's mother stayed upstairs, too distraught to face meeting me.

In 2010 I was contacted by Marc Hall, an Englishman who was conducting research into the massive Operation Hurricane raids on Duisburg and other German cities that were carried out by the RAF on the night of 14/15 October 1944 when Ron and I were shot down. As part of Operation Hurricane there were big attacks on Duisburg (two raids of 675 and 330 aircraft respectively) and Brunswick (240 aircraft), and smaller raids from Mosquitoes on Hamburg, Düsseldorf, Mannheim and Berlin. Approximately 10,050 tonnes of bombs were dropped in twenty-four hours – a total never exceeded during the war. The Bomber Command log entry for the night concludes by commenting triumphantly:

The whole air defence system of the Reich must have reverberated with echoes of the failure that it suffered on this night – a failure without parallel. The lesson the enemy may draw from it may well be that without an adequate system of early warning it is impossible to maintain his night fighter forces around the western circumference of his territory, and that more defence in depth will be necessary to guard his interior, even if it leaves the Ruhr and Middle Rhine more vulnerable. On this night he was badly taken by surprise in the centre of his 400 mile arc, and so badly spoofed on the northern and southern sectors that he failed altogether to deal with a serious deep penetration to Brunswick. Our losses on the two raids on Duisburg, and on Brunswick, were in each case very much lower than ever before: 'bomber support' was more elaborate than had been previously attempted.

It is somewhat ironic that notwithstanding the self-congratulatory tone of this entry, the operations it describes proved to be fatal for my friend Ron and very nearly for me too.

Marc Hall had discovered that my Mosquito

231

had come down five miles south-east of Munster and that German records suggested a body had been found in the wreckage, but never identified. I'm not sure why, but Ron didn't wear identity tags – maybe this was just superstition, or whether there was another reason – perhaps he was Jewish?

The Prinzens
Shortly after the war the Prinzens' farmhouse was burnt to the ground. They received some insurance money, but rather than rebuild they decided to emigrate with their children to Canada where they had relatives. Only the eldest daughter, Truida, stayed behind and with her husband built a new farmhouse near the site of Samsonhuis. She lived there until very recently, when she moved into a nursing home. The remainder of the Prinzen family relocated to a farming area near Toronto where they initially worked as farm labourers until they had enough money to buy their own farms. They were very successful farmers and all did well in their new country. I visited them a couple of times in Canada. I was very touched that when Mother Prinzen was very ill she asked to see me and I was able to travel to be with her for a few days before she died.

Joe Davis
Joe became a lieutenant colonel in the US Air Force and had a very successful career. He died relatively young of a brain tumour, and was never able to take up a posting to the Pentagon.

Bobby Brown

Bobby worked as a plumber in his own company after the war and I visited him in his home in San Francisco. Unfortunately he became terminally ill with cancer, but with assistance from Prince Bernhard and KLM, Long Henk and I were able to arrange for Jan to visit him shortly before he died in 1963.

Owen Mayberry

I visited Owen in the US, where he worked for the Government, and subsequently at Aerojet in a job assembling rocket parts. Owen's wife Doris wrote about his experiences hiding at the Prinzens in a book published privately in 1995. In retirement Owen became a guide in the local rail museum in Sacramento.

Ted Roblee

Owen maintained some contact with Ted after the war, but it was apparent that Ted was affected by his wartime experiences and wanted to leave them behind and not be reminded of that period. On leaving the USAAF he went to college before joining the farm equipment manufacturer Allis-Chalmers where he had a successful career selling agricultural machinery.

Jim Strickland

Jim returned to Australia and set up his own business in Melbourne, specialising in fitting out school classrooms. He later went into real estate and retired to Queensland. When I travelled to see my own family in Australia, Isabel and I always visited Jim; he was a great extrovert and a lot of fun to be with.

Chuck Huntley
Chuck had a full career as a pilot in the Royal Canadian Air Force. He later ran a bar and hotel in British Columbia before eventually retiring there.

Jan Ket
When we were liberated, Jan and his team of ninety partisans were given the job of clearing German resistance on either side of the armoured thrust eastwards to free the remainder of the Netherlands. They became a unit of the Canadian Army and Jan had to exchange his extraordinary guerrilla costume for a Canadian uniform. After the liberation and surrender of the German armies in the Netherlands Jan was put in charge of 2,500 German prisoners of war, whom he characteristically set to work clearing German minefields. Jan was formally transferred into the Dutch Army and sent out to the Far East to fight Indonesian nationalists in what had been the Dutch East Indies.

He was in Indonesia when I returned to Holland in 1946 and I did not see him for another ten years. When we did meet up I briefly discussed the episode with the German soldiers at De Berk and I said to him, 'I concede there was no other alternative to what you ordered.' After the Dutch left Indonesia, Jan stayed with the Dutch Army. Because of his training in the Navy Jan was very competent in engineering matters and became an

Army engineer. Towards the end of his career he was in charge of the REME workshops at the Dutch Army base at Soestdijk, and he retired with the rank of major and with many decorations, including the Bronzen Leeuw (Bronze Lion), one of the highest Dutch military awards.

In the 1970s I heard from Long Henk that Jan was dying, so together we went to visit him. He told me that he had a lot of guns and ammunition that he thought would be difficult for his wife to get rid of after he died. I went up to the attic of his house and found an arsenal of Bren guns, Sten guns and rifles that he'd been keeping against the day the Russians tried to invade the Netherlands. I helped him shift these to Long Henk's house.

Long Henk
Following the liberation of Aalten, Long Henk was wounded fighting the Germans with Jan's resistance unit. The local hospital did not have a bed long enough for him to lie down in so he and his colleagues took a truck and went into Germany and stole one! Later, after he had recovered from his wounds, he went with Jan to fight in the Dutch Army in the Dutch East Indies.

When the war there ended he left the Dutch Army and became a business consultant before working for a large department store chain called Bijenkorf. He sat on the Bijenkorf Board and was responsible for finding sites for their new stores. I stayed close to Henk after the war and our families frequently visited each other and became good friends. Henk was a tough chap in the dark days of conflict and his character remained formed by his wartime experiences; he took no nonsense in family or business life. Some time after Jan's death, Henk himself fell ill with cancer and we had to decide what to do with all the guns and ammunition that we had retrieved from Jan. Eventually we found a former resistance fighter who was now a superintendent of police, and he was able to help us dispose of the weapons in a legal manner.

Ben te Brinke

After the British forces crossed the Rhine in March 1945, Ben climbed down below a bridge over a tributary of the Rhine at Aalten and cut the electric wires that were intended to detonate explosives the Germans had laid to blow the bridge up to cover their retreat. After the war I once stayed with Jan and went to visit Ben, who had remained in farming.

Wilheim and Daatje Hoftizer

Wilheim survived his spell in a German labour camp but came back at the end of the war a shadow of his former self. But he was still capable of running his farm and business and he and Daatje attended my wedding in 1946, along with Bernard and Dora Prinzen. Wilheim was joined in his contracting business by his sons and it became very successful. Later Daatje came to the UK with a group of Dutch helpers, hosted by the Escaping Society, and I was able to meet up with her again.

Bob Kroll

During the time I was in Holland I never knew exactly who Bob was and where he fitted into the Resistance organisation. Subsequently I realised that he was a senior person to whom Jan reported. Presumably he in turn was answerable to Prince Bernhard, the head of the Dutch Resistance, who was then based with the Allied armies in Tilburg. In 1995 a party of Dutch people from the Aalten area, including Bob Kroll, was invited to London by the Escaping Society to mark the fiftieth anniversary of the ending of the war in Europe, and to enable us to express our undying thanks to these remarkable people for all they had done to enable airmen to return home safely. I did not have an opportunity to meet with him during this visit and was later told that he returned to Holland in tears, not having been recognised for all that he had done and the dangers he had survived. The sad fact of the matter was that at the time no one had known of his activities. I'm now troubled that his contribution may not have been recognised, perhaps because he subsequently fell out with Jan and Long Henk. I suspect this dispute was over the events at De Berk when Jan felt he did not receive Bob's support in dealing with the impossible situation in which he found himself.

Chapter 23

Reflections

Of course war is cruel and arbitrary. I saw many instances where simple bad luck had tragic consequences – Ron in the nose of the Mosquito separated from his parachute; the Dutch doctor who saved my life shot up in his car by an Allied plane; and the German lieutenant looking for a billet stumbling across a barn occupied by the Resistance. I was lucky in many respects, but had my share of traumatic events too. As a result, memories of these times have never gone away and I consciously decided to deal with them by sharing my experiences. Not long after I returned from Holland I wrote down my account of being shot down and on the run in Germany, and subsequently I talked about what had happened to me with my family and friends.

I think that I matured quickly as a result of my wartime circumstances. Flying with Bomber Command had its challenges, but the really testing aspect was what occurred after I was shot down. In Holland, I always felt that it was important that what one did would reflect well on Britain and the RAF. I thought the Dutch demanded a lot of me as a RAF officer and I was determined to live up to their expectations to the best of my ability. In such a mixture of backgrounds and nationalities, leadership had to be earned and was not gifted to one.

I was very conscious of all the help given to me by very humble people, such as the farmers who hid me, and this made me appreciate what marvellous people there are at all levels of society. I probably had the prejudices of a middle-class upbringing and public school education before the war, and when I was in hiding I found that it was often the people at the bottom of society who took the highest risks and made the greatest contribution in resisting the Germans. I'm a more respectful person as a result of my experiences in Holland and this influenced my attitude in later years, even in the airline world, where I hope I had a more sympathetic perspective than some to people doing unassuming jobs in the company. I would like to think that I listened to the concerns and worries of those for whom I was responsible and acted justly.

The Bomber Command strategy has always been controversial. Before the Second World War nobody had tested the philosophy of trying to win the war by bombing the enemy's cities. I remember the impact of the German bombing of London and especially Coventry, and Bomber Harris's quotation from the Old Testament: 'They have sown the wind, they will reap the whirlwind.' In my judgement, abhorrent although it sounds, this did prove to be a successful strategy overall. The German Armaments Minister, Albert Speer, said that if the RAF had been able to repeat what happened to Hamburg in 1943 within three months, then Germany would have surrendered. I think that this is what actually happened in Japan where the Tokyo firestorm caused by conventional bombing (the most terrible of the Second World War in terms of loss of life), followed by the atomic bombs in Hiroshima and Nagasaki, forced the Japanese to surrender.

Although the outcome was successful generally, I am saddened by the civilian casualties that were an inevitable consequence of bombing German cities. However, in the years between Dunkirk and D-Day the only way open for Britain to strike back in Europe was to send over to Germany the greatest bomber fleet that they could muster. This was understood by the civilians in the Netherlands who could see by day and hear by night great numbers of aircraft forcing their way into the maelstrom of fire over the Fatherland, and time after time witnessed the tragedy of planes being shot down. I never heard the Dutch question the consequences of this strategy even though there were sometimes civilian casualties in the Netherlands. The Dutch wanted to see Germany smashed and the Allied aircrew who were endeavouring to bring this about were held in the greatest esteem for what they were doing. When they could help our airmen they did so immediately and unstintingly, and when tragically any were beyond their help, they were given a decent burial in the local churchyard and their graves were tended and marked with flowers.

I am very conscious of the huge loss of British aircrew – over 55,000 perished in the hostilities, more than the number of British Army officers who were killed in the First World War. I have a photograph of my football team at prep school. About half the team died during the war. So many of my friends from the Air Force did not survive. While I was held back to work as an instructor, most of those on my training course in the United States returned to Britain and arrived back to fly with Bomber Command in 1943 at a time when the odds were stacked against their survival.

I feel critical of the way the heavy casualties came about. Many of the British aircraft in the early part of the war were death traps for the men who flew them, and even bombers like the Lancasters were shockingly vulnerable to German fighters – I will always remember the sickening sight of seeing burning planes dropping out of the sky when I was on the ground in the Netherlands, and this was at a late stage in the war when it was clear that the RAF had won the air war. With hindsight, it would have been preferable to have used many more Mosquitoes – with a crew of just two, but carrying a relatively large bomb load of 4,000 pounds – rather than sending over Lancasters and Halifaxes and other heavy bombers with seven crew members each.

I am also very disappointed by the treatment after the war of those who flew with Bomber Command. Even politicians like Churchill who were involved in agreeing Bomber Command's strategies subsequently distanced themselves from them. Bomber Harris was the only one of the wartime British commanders never to be made a peer. Given the risks that flyers of Bomber Command took I believe they deserved better official recognition. I now live in Sydney, Australia, and flew across the world to attend the unveiling by the Queen of the Bomber Command Memorial in Green Park on 28 June 2012. I wanted to do this to recognise my friend Ron and all the others of Bomber Command who did not survive the war. It was a sombre occasion in many respects and it is difficult to put into words what I felt. As well as the grief of the families and friends for the individuals who died, I think that Britain suffered grievously from the loss of the aircrew. Their deaths were a national tragedy and their absence had a serious effect on Britain's post-war life.

Appendix I

Glossary and Acronyms

ATC: Air Traffic Control.

The Big City: Slang for Berlin.

Boozer light: Two small radio receivers, one tuned to the German ground radar frequency and connected to an amber warning light, and the other tuned to the German night-fighter radar frequency and connected to a red warning light. The amber light would come on when the ground radar engaged with the aircraft and the red light would come on when the fighter aircraft's radar joined with the aircraft.

Drem: A lighting system surrounding an airfield with a ring of lights and a mile radius around the airfield with a gap at both ends in line with the runway, named after the Drem RAF station in East Lothian, Scotland, where the lighting system was first developed.

DUKW: A six-wheel-drive amphibious truck used by the United States and British military during the Second World War.

F/O: Flying Officer.

G-box operators: Slang for navigators who operated the Gee navigation system.

Gee: A navigation system used by the RAF involving radio transmitter stations in England sending pulses which, when received by the bomber aircraft, allowed the aircraft to plot its position.

H2S: An airborne ground scanning radar used by the RAF.

High blower: Known as such when the Mosquito's supercharger was switched to high above 20,000 feet so that it blew a greater amount of petrol into the engine, causing the aircraft's speed to increase.

Intelligence King: The squadron's intelligence officer.

ITMA: *It's That Man Again,* a BBC radio comedy show which ran from 1939 to 1949.

ITW: Initial Training Wing; the basic military training that RAF personnel did prior to going on to Elementary Flying Training School. This basic training involved a lot of military drill.

Jane: A cartoon strip in the *Daily Mirror* that

featured the heroine Jane losing her clothing in a variety of unlikely situations.

LNSF: Light Night Striking Force; squadrons of Mosquitoes, forming part of the Pathfinders, used for carrying out bomber raids as a diversion to the 'main force' of heavy bombers.

MI9: Military Intelligence Section 9, a department of British Military Intelligence, responsible for recovering British soldiers or aircrew from behind enemy lines. They also provided training on how to survive in hostile territory, and for the contents of the escape kits that we carried with us and that were so important for me when I found myself shot down.

NAAFI: The Navy, Army and Air Force Institutes, an organisation that ran clubs, bars, shops and other facilities on British military bases and sold goods to servicemen.

NSB: Nationaal-Socialistische Beweging, otherwise known as the Dutch Nazi Party.

Oboe: A navigation system used by the RAF. A bomber flew along a circle of electronic pulses defined by one transmitting station in England – known as the 'Cat' – and dropped its load (either bombs or marking flares, depending on the mission) when it reached the intersection with the circle defined by another station, known as 'Mouse'.

OTC: Officer Training Corps; a programme at some schools (particularly public schools like Dover College), training students to become officers in the armed forces.

Pathfinders: Elite squadrons of the RAF used for marking targets and undertaking diversionary raids.

P/O: Pilot Officer.

RAAF: Royal Australian Air Force, formed in March 1921.

RAF: Royal Air Force, the British service founded in April 1918.

RFC: Royal Flying Corps; the air arm of the British Army during the First World War, prior to the formation of the RAF.

Seyss-Inquart, Arthur: An Austrian who served as the Reichskommissar (Governor) of Holland during the Nazi Occupation from 1940 to 1945. He was tried for war crimes at the Nuremberg Trials and executed in 1946.

SOE: Special Operations Executive, a British Government department, established by Churchill to assist resistance organisations in carrying out guerrilla warfare and clandestine operations in enemy-occupied countries.

Standard Beam Approach (SBA): Radio

beam system aligned with the runway for use in bad visibility and at night.

USAAF: United States Army Air Forces, the US air service between 1941 and 1947.

WAAC (later WAC): Women's Army Auxiliary Corps; a women-only unit of the US Army established during the Second World War.

WAAF: Women's Auxiliary Air Force; a women-only unit of the Royal Air Force established during the Second World War.

Appendix II

De Havilland Mosquito Specification

Type: Twin-engined two-man mid-wing mono-plane bomber.

Powerplant: Mk I and IV, two 1,460hp Rolls-Royce Merlin 21, 22 or 25 12-cylinder liquid-cooled supercharged in-line engines; Mk IX and XVI, two 1,680 hp Merlin 72 and 73 or 1,710hp Merlin 76 and 77 engines.

Dimensions: Span 54ft 2in, length 40ft 6in, height 12ft 6in, wing area 454 sq ft.

Weights: Mk IV, empty 13,400lb, loaded 21,462lb; Mk IX, empty 14,570lb, loaded 22,780lb.

Performance: Mk IV, max speed 380mph at 17,000ft, service ceiling 29,100ft, range 2,100 miles. Mk XVI, max speed 415mph at 28,000ft, service ceiling 37,000ft range with max bomb load 1,485 miles.

Armament: Defensive: none. Offensive: Mk IV,

max bomb load 2,000lb; Mk IX and XVI, max bomb load 4,000lb, plus 2 x 500lb bombs under wings.

Production: 7,781 of which 1,690 were completed as unarmed bombers.

Source: Falconer, J. Bomber Command Handbook 1939–1945 (Sutton Publishing 2003)

Endnotes

1 The 'Gap' was an area that represented a space between the defences of the Ruhr and the defences of the west to east line of cities between Münster and Berlin.

2 'Paramatta' involved ground-marking flares as opposed to 'Wanganui' sky markers.

3 Ron had a list of code names for RAF stations, which were typed on rice paper and meant to be swallowed if we ever came down over enemy territory.

4 Figures cited by Max Hastings in *Bomber Command* (1999 edn), P. 286.

5 Hastings, op. cit., P. 299.

6 Ground markers were code named 'Paramatta' and sky markers were code named 'Wanganui'. We would be advised in advance whether Wanganui or Paramatta markers would be used, depending on whether cloud cover was expected – I can only recall Wanganui sky markers being employed on one or two occasions.

7 Twenty years later I was involved in implementing the same technique in the airline business.

8 Years later I was stuck in a traffic jam at the Hammersmith flyover in London and I heard the same music on the car radio. When I got home I phoned the BBC and found out that the haunting music I'd heard was 'Va Pensiero' the Chorus of the Hebrew Slaves, from the opera *Nabucco* by Giuseppe Verdi.

9 A type of beet.

10 Dutch for 'quiet'.

11 This was Grys van Haaften, who I subsequently was able to meet again after the war.

12 Figures quoted in M.R.D. Foot and J.M. Langley, *MI9 Escape and Evasion 1939–1945* (1979).

We do hope that you have enjoyed reading this large print book.

Did you know that all of our titles are available for purchase?

We publish a wide range of high quality large print books including:
Romances, Mysteries, Classics
General Fiction
Non Fiction and Westerns

Special interest titles available in large print are:
The Little Oxford Dictionary
Music Book
Song Book
Hymn Book
Service Book

Also available from us courtesy of Oxford University Press:
Young Readers' Dictionary
(large print edition)
Young Readers' Thesaurus
(large print edition)

For further information or a free brochure, please contact us at:
Ulverscroft Large Print Books Ltd.,
The Green, Bradgate Road, Anstey,
Leicester, LE7 7FU, England.
Tel: (00 44) 0116 236 4325
Fax: (00 44) 0116 234 0205

Other titles published by Ulverscroft:

IF THE CAP FITS

Steve Halliwell

Steve Halliwell is best known as the loveable patriarch Zak Dingle in the hit TV show Emmerdale, a part he has played since 1994. He is now one of the UK's most recognisable and treasured soap stars. Yet before his success, Halliwell spent many years desperately seeking work, and even spent time on the streets. This warts-and-all story of his rise to fame is an inspiration. It explores the wider class history that permeated the country in the sixties and seventies and still lingers today. Above all, it is an honest tale of rejection and redemption and will appeal to all who have the ambition to better themselves.